Global Supply Chain Management

Global Supply Chain Management

Matt Drake, PhD, CFPIM

Director of International Business Programs
Assistant Professor of Supply Chain Management
Duquesne University

First published in 2011 by
Business Expert Press, LLC
222 East 46th Street, New York, NY 10017
www.businessexpertpress.com

ISBN-13: 978-1-60649-276-5 (paperback)
ISBN-13: 978-1-60649-277-2 (e-book)

10.4128/9781606492772

A publication in the Business Expert Press Supply and Operations Management collection

Collection ISSN: 2156-8189 (print)
Collection ISSN: 2156-8200 (electronic)

Cover design by Jonathan Pennell
Interior design by Scribe Inc.

First edition: January 2012

10 9 8 7 6 5 4 3 2 1

Printed in the United States of America.

For my wife, Nicole, whose love gives me the strength to persevere through any difficulties that I encounter. I could not have written this book without you.

Abstract

The business environment in the twenty-first century is truly global in scope. Companies must navigate and manage networks of international suppliers and customers to compete in a global marketplace. An efficient and effective supply chain can provide a sustainable competitive advantage that will secure a firm's position in the global market. Global supply chains are often fraught with complexity and uncertainty that make them difficult to manage in a way that enables the firm to realize the maximum potential advantage. Executives and managers at all levels will come to appreciate the importance of supply chain management to their firm's overall performance and competitiveness. This book will illustrate the challenges of managing a global supply chain and will discuss cutting-edge strategies that firms can use to cope with these challenges and improve their supply chain performance. Particular topics of interest include supply chain risk management, the total cost of ownership approach to procurement, global supplier selection, network orchestration, transportation and distribution strategies around the world, and transportation security measures. Each chapter also includes brief case studies that illustrate concepts and techniques in action within specific company environments.

Keywords

Supply chain management, international business, global sourcing, risk management, international logistics

Contents

Acknowledgments

I would like to thank my editor, Steven Nahmias, at Business Expert Press who believed in this project from the moment that I pitched it to him. My production liaison, Cindy Durand, provided me with all the details I needed to know to process my manuscript smoothly. I am also indebted to John Mawhinney and Bill Presutti, my colleagues in the supply chain management department at Duquesne University, who reviewed previous versions of this manuscript and contributed their insightful comments. They have helped to improve this book immensely, and any errors that still exist in this text should be attributed to me alone.

CHAPTER 1

What Is Supply Chain Management?

As I sit and listen to the seemingly interminable honks of the cars and auto-rickshaws outside of my hotel room in Kottayam, India, I cannot help but reflect on how small the world has become in the past few decades. You cannot go anywhere in India without seeing signs of the Western world in the form of cars, electronics, billboard advertisements, and the like. Even in the small town of Thekkady, nestled high in the Western Ghats mountain range, I could purchase Lay's potato chips or Aquafina water if I desired.

A major mechanism behind this shrinking of the world is the development of global supply chain networks designed to manufacture and move products to every corner of the world. With the proliferation of international air travel and the improvement of logistics infrastructure around the world, it is now possible to catch a fish in the Mediterranean Sea or in the waters off the coast of Prince Edward Island and feast on that same fish in a Tokyo sushi bar several days later.[1] A product manufactured deep in the interior of China could be delivered direct to a customer in the American heartland within the week. This is the state of world-class supply chain management in the twenty-first century.

Of course, few products are able to navigate the complex web of international trade regulations and domestic distribution operations so quickly and seamlessly. Much of the logistics infrastructure around the world is underdeveloped. The two-lane road that my hotel sits on in Kottayam has to handle traffic in the form of cars, pedestrians, bicycles, auto-rickshaws, motorcycles, buses, trucks, and even elephants! The road system in India is very poor; in most places, two-lane roads are the largest that you will see. A road can go from pavement to dirt in an instant, causing havoc for cars, let alone trucks carrying goods. I cannot even imagine taking a 53-foot trailer that is at home on the U.S. Interstate Highway System on these roads with traffic weaving in and out. If the goods actually arrived at their destination safely, chances are there would be no adequate dock to unload the freight. India is not alone with its infrastructure issues; many other countries have roads and ports that are not conducive to hauling large quantities of freight on a consistent basis.

Thus even if we can say that the world is smaller, this does not mean that it is completely homogeneous. There are plenty of differences in culture, economic and political policies, regulations, and physical and climatic characteristics that complicate efforts to manage a global supply chain. When a company operates (i.e., with respect to procurement, manufacturing, and distribution) entirely within the boundaries of one country, its supply chain managers only have to worry about the domestic regulations and culture they live with everyday. Very few companies outside of those that tout themselves as selling or producing "locally sourced" products can say with any certainty that they have a truly domestic supply chain.[2] Most companies today are explicitly tied to the global marketplace and, as a consequence, have a global supply chain.

The complexities related to managing global supply chains can cause firms great difficulties and can even make decisions that look sound on paper (such as offshoring work to another country or entering a foreign market) turn out to be unprofitable. They can also, however, provide an opportunity for organizations to establish a strong competitive advantage by learning how to manage the issues that trip up other firms. This book is designed to highlight the importance of managing global supply chains effectively, as well as to provide insight and recommendations for handling the most important obstacles to making your supply chain successful in the global marketplace.

Supply Chain Management Defined

Before we delve too far into the challenges of global supply chain management, it is important in this first chapter that we take some time to examine *supply chain management* itself, for this is a term that has been used in many different contexts in the business vernacular and can cause confusion as a result.

Supply chain management as a field is approximately 25 years old, but the traditional business functions that compose it (i.e., procurement, forecasting, production, transportation, warehousing, customer service, order management) have been around since business began. The Council of Supply Chain Management Professionals (CSCMP) defines *supply chain management* as

> encompass[ing] the planning and management of all activities involved in sourcing and procurement, conversion, and all logistics management activities. Importantly it also includes coordination and collaboration with channel partners, which can be suppliers, intermediaries, third-party service providers, and customers. In essence, Supply Chain Management integrates supply and demand management within and across companies.[3]

The most important part of this definition is its emphasis on the interorganizational element of supply chain management. This is what sets supply chain management apart from its traditional business functions and its predecessors of materials management, physical distribution, and business logistics. True supply chain management focuses on interactions and collaboration with suppliers and customers to ensure that the end customer's requirements are satisfied adequately. All activities in the supply chain should be undertaken with the customer's requirements in mind; all supply chains ultimately exist to ensure that the customers are satisfied.

Both academic and practitioner discussions of supply chain management inevitably include some specialized terminology to describe a firm's position in the supply chain relative to its partners. In the "chain" part of the supply chain metaphor, suppliers are referred to as *upstream* entities, and customers are called *downstream* entities. The firm's immediate suppliers are *tier 1* suppliers, their suppliers are *tier 2* suppliers, and so on. The same vernacular is used to describe the different echelons of customers all the way down to the end customer. In this way it has often been said that supply chain management seeks to coordinate operations from the "supplier's supplier to the customer's customer."

The Supply Chain Council, an international nonprofit dedicated to helping organizations improve their supply chain performance, has developed its widely applied Supply Chain Operations Reference (SCOR®) process reference model to align a firm's supply chain performance metrics with its overall strategic goals.[4] It is helpful to consider the SCOR® model's highest level processes when describing supply chain management:

Example 1.1. Co-Creating Value With Customers

As firms adopt a supply chain perspective and consider their inter-actions with suppliers and customers, they can often differentiate themselves in the market by engaging customers in the value creation process. This is a concept known as *co-creation*. In many traditional supply chains, the customers themselves play little role in creating value; they only consume the value that the manufacturers create. Many firms, from gas stations and grocery stores to Ikea, have designed ways for customers to create their own value through gas pumps, self-checkout machines, and furniture that is assembled at home.

A more significant way to have customers create value is to involve them in the manufacturer's product design process. In the industrial context customers' representatives from procurement and engineering can work with the manufacturer to collaborate on a design that meets their needs. Many consumer product manufacturers such as Lego and Nike have established online design studios where customers can customize their own offerings to meet their needs. Many college textbook publishers offer customized textbooks where faculty members can select chapters from several textbooks along with additional readings to design their own textbook that fits their courses better than the general textbook offerings can. Even retailers such as Amazon and Walmart invite their customers to rate and comment on the products they purchase online to provide additional guidance for future customers.

Source: Prahalad and Ramaswamy (2004).

1. *Plan.* All supply chains must undertake a significant amount of planning because so many of their operations are performed in different locations and most of the time in different companies' facilities. It takes a great deal of planning to synchronize these actions, and this synchronization is important because the activities are cross-functional and interrelated.
2. *Source.* After the initial plans have been established, the firm starts to acquire resources from its suppliers, often in the form of parts or partially manufactured subassemblies, but this can also include resources such as machinery, technology, capacity, and other services.

3. *Make.* Once the resources have been acquired, the firm performs its primary transformation activity to turn resource inputs into outputs that can ultimately satisfy downstream demands from other members of the supply chain or the end customer.

4. *Deliver.* After the resources are transformed from inputs to outputs, they must be moved physically to the next phase of distribution. If the output item is a part, it must be delivered to another manufacturer who will use it as an input. If the output item is a finished item that can be sold to the end customer, the item is delivered to the next layer of distribution (e.g., central warehouse or retail store). The delivery of services requires that the firm manage its customer requirements and ensure that the customer is satisfied with the service received.

5. *Return.* The original SCOR® model stopped at the deliver process, but the Supply Chain Council appended the model in the early 2000s to acknowledge that products often flow in the reverse direction from the traditional flow for a variety of reasons (e.g., defects, shipment errors, buyback arrangements, customer service policies, or end-of-life disposal). These return flows can be very costly for companies that have not developed appropriate processes to handle them, and they can turn into a revenue source and competitive advantage for companies that proactively plan for them.

Implicit in the SCOR® model's description of a firm's supply chain processes are the linkages of these processes with those of the firm's supply chain partners. For example, a manufacturer's sourcing process is invariably dependent on its suppliers' delivery processes. The SCOR® model explicitly shows how companies in the same supply chain are linked and gives managers a map of them so that none of the linkages are overlooked, which could lead to a breakdown in the entire chain.

The Evolution of Supply Chain Management

This section describes some important factors and milestones in the development of the supply chain management field over the past century. This is not meant to be an exhaustive history, however, because that would fill an entire book on its own.

The field of supply chain management has its origins in the giant manufacturing firms of the late nineteenth century. It was common for large firms in that era to own many or all of the stages of production from raw materials to finished goods and even part of the distribution channel as well. Ford Motor Company is the classic example of such an approach, which is called *vertical integration*. In the 1920s Ford owned its main manufacturing facility in River Rouge, Michigan, but it also owned rubber plantations, glassworks, railroads, forests and timber operations, coal and iron ore mines, and ocean carriers.[5]

The main benefit to complete vertical integration is the degree of control that a firm has over its supply chain operations. The more stages of a supply chain that a firm owns, the easier it is for the firm to coordinate the operations to minimize waste in the form of excess inventory buffers. The downside, though, is that the firm must be able to perform all of these functions well and synchronize them so that they occur in a timely manner. As the twentieth century progressed, most vertically integrated firms divested themselves of their ancillary functions and processes to focus on their core competencies, the functions that positively distinguish a firm from its competitors.

In the 1960s the major business functions related to supply chain management, such as procurement, forecasting, production, transportation, and warehousing, all operated independently in what have become known as *functional silos*.[6] Employees in each of these departments made decisions with only their department's interests in mind and without concern for how their decisions affected other departments' ability to satisfy the end customer's demand.[7]

In the 1970s many firms began to recognize that these business functions are inherently linked and dependent upon each other and started to manage them together, as a group. All of a firm's inbound activities to the point of production were grouped under the header "materials management," while the outbound activities after production of a good were called "physical distribution." It should not be difficult to see where the trend went from this point.

In the 1980s firms established the link between the inbound materials management processes and the outbound physical distribution processes under the heading "integrated business logistics." Firms that truly integrated their logistics processes managed all the processes involved with sourcing, making, and delivering products together, but it was not until the late 1980s and early 1990s that the focus shifted outside of the company's internal operations and functions and to the firm's interactions with suppliers and customers. Supply chain management as we know it today began when firms recognized that, regardless of where they stood in the supply chain hierarchy, they should be focused on satisfying the end users of their products and services, and their ability to fulfill customers' demands was necessarily dependent on the performance of their suppliers (and their suppliers' suppliers).

It is no coincidence that this timeline of business process coordination and channel collaboration mirrors the development of business enterprise and communications information technology. Supply chain management is inherently dependent on technology to facilitate the sharing of information between partners and coordination of actions between parties that are likely located many miles from each other. The gains from such coordination and joint planning would be severely limited without the ability to share information and communicate quickly and easily. Any supply chain that does not perform tasks entirely inside one physical building (which is all supply chains) must have some minimum level of proximity in relation to geographic, organizational, cultural, or electronic characteristics to be effective; this proximity is often easiest to accomplish through the deployment of information and communications systems.[8]

The development of the supply chain management field was influenced by the discovery by Procter & Gamble (P&G) of the phenomenon known as the *bullwhip effect*.[9] Managers at P&G could not understand the data that they had investigated with respect to their Pampers brand of diapers. If any product should have relatively constant demand at the retail store level over the course of a year, it should be diapers. There are no predictable seasonal fluctuations as there are for, say, snow blowers, and the market demand does not grow or decline very quickly over time (unless P&G were able to successfully capture market share from its competitors). As a result, it should be no surprise that the managers were puzzled to see a graph of the orders they received from their wholesalers and large retailers exhibited a great deal of variability. Some weeks the orders from a customer would be very high, and the next week they would drop off precipitously. There had to be a reason that they were experiencing such a counterintuitive result.

After investigating order data from every level of the distribution channel for the diapers, the researchers identified a pattern that they found also held true for other products. As orders moved further upstream in the supply chain (toward the manufacturer), the variability of the orders increased. End-user demand at the retail-store level was indeed relatively flat, but the orders that the stores placed to the retailer's distribution center were more variable. The pattern of increasing variability continued until the orders reached P&G, the manufacturer.

In the work that followed, the researchers were able to identify the following four major causes of the bullwhip effect:

1. *Demand forecast updating.* This is the major cause of the bullwhip effect, and it stems from a lack of information sharing in the supply chain. If upstream entities (such as P&G) are not able to see the end customers' demand at the retail level, they have no choice but to base their demand forecast on the orders that they see from their immediate customers (i.e., wholesalers and large retailers). These orders already have more variability than the actual demand does, and the forecasting process adds another layer of error because forecasts are never 100% accurate over time. Every time an entity has to forecast based on channel partner orders instead of on actual end customer demand, variability increases. This effect can be mitigated by engaging the retailer to share the end customer demand for the product, which is captured by their point-of-sale scanning systems, so that the upstream parties can use this information to plan their production instead of relying on forecasts of a wholesaler's orders. While demand forecast updating is the main cause of the bullwhip effect, the latter cannot be entirely eliminated just by sharing point-of-sale demand information because of the subsequent causes of the bullwhip effect.

2. *Order batching.* When order setup costs are large, companies have an incentive to order larger quantities than they actually need so that they can avoid paying the setup cost so often. These larger orders introduce variability into the ordering pattern experienced by the supplier because a customer may order many units 1 week and then none for the next 3 or 4 weeks, even if their actual requirements for the product are constant each week. This is a more variable pattern than it would be if the firm ordered exactly what it needed each week. Suppliers often react to this variable ordering pattern by

holding a large amount of inventory because they find it difficult to predict when the large order will be placed. Customers can help the supplier improve performance by providing visibility to their real-time inventory levels. By monitoring the inventory levels, the supplier can easily see when a large order is likely to be placed.

3. *Price fluctuations.* Firms will often offer short-term or quantity discounts on their products as a way to entice customers to purchase more. They may not realize it, but these discounts can actually introduce variability into the demand that they see from their customers. If customers decide to purchase more than they actually need and store it for subsequent periods, the supplier experiences the same result as in the order-batching case. Consistent pricing policies devoid of discounts incentivize the customers to purchase only what they need instead of stocking up to take advantage of a discount. This is the crux of Walmart's famous "Everyday Low Prices" policy. Walmart smartly used this policy as a marketing strategy as well, but it was mainly designed to mitigate the variability in demand that it experienced from its customers.

4. *Shortage gaming.* If customers know a supplier is going to be short on capacity for a given period, which is what the Japanese automakers experienced in the summer of 2011 as a result of the earthquake and tsunami that rocked Japan earlier that year, it is extremely important for the supplier to allocate the scarce supply smartly. If the supplier uses a policy such as a common percentage to fulfill customer orders (where each customer will receive X% of their actual units ordered), then customers have the incentive to inflate their orders artificially in the hope that they ultimately receive their desired amount. If the supplier looks at the actual orders received later on to forecast demand in the future, this could lead to an erroneous estimate because the large orders were due only to the allocation mechanism and not to an increase in demand. In this case, an allocation mechanism based on *past* orders would be more appropriate to eliminate this gaming strategy.[10]

A common thread throughout the causes of the bullwhip effect is the misalignment of decentralized decision makers within the supply chain. Like it or not, employees often make decisions to take advantage of the incentives that they face at the time, and these incentives are not always aligned with the interests of the supply chain as a whole. Hau Lee identified the three important components of creating the "Triple-A Supply Chain," and incentive alignment was one of the three major foci that can help firms create a world-class supply chain.[11] Lee cites misaligned incentives with contract manufacturers as the main reason for Cisco's US$2.25 billion inventory write-off in 2001. Incentive alignment efforts begin with sharing information between supply chain partners, but they also often include mechanisms that redistribute risks, rewards, or both among the channel members. Some popular examples of incentive alignment mechanisms in supply chains include buyback agreements, revenue-sharing arrangements, and quantity-flexibility contracts.[12]

Of course, it is impossible for a company to align its incentives with those of its overall supply chain if the firm does not have its own internal business functions aligned. There are many stories of companies in which production is at odds with marketing, and engineering is constantly fighting with purchasing, even from companies that are often viewed as leaders in supply chain management. A recent survey of operations and sales employees in a large Europe-based multinational group with many different brands in its product portfolio showed significant gaps between the interests and priorities of those employees in sales and those in operations. In fact, the only item both departments agreed upon was the importance of working toward internal realignment.[13] Another recent study found that internal alignment is a positive predictor of the success of efforts to integrate with suppliers or customers and that these successful external integration efforts enhance an organization's competitive capabilities and, subsequently, its financial performance.[14]

The issue of internal misalignment is not necessarily restricted to the functional areas. A particular business function's incentives could be misaligned with the strategic goals of the organization as a whole. Consider the following simple example. A manufacturing plant manager's quarterly bonus is largely based on plant utilization over the quarter. At first glance, this may seem to be a perfectly reasonable metric because most firms would like to have high utilization of their capital equipment. To maximize utilization, however, it would be in the manager's best interest to have the plant running for as much time as possible, constantly producing goods whether there is demand for those goods or not. In its most critical realization, the manager would produce only one type of product for the entire quarter, effectively running the plant like a paper mill or an oil refinery, to avoid any downtime related to changeovers. It is important to monitor metrics such as utilization, but they should not be considered myopically. They must be combined with other metrics related to customer service and asset turnover to ensure that the plant operates in accordance with the firm's overall competitive strategy. The senior managers at the European firm where the survey was conducted were floored to see that some of their strategic initiatives were viewed as having little importance in the eyes of many of their surveyed employees.[15]

Example 1.2. Synchronizing the Supply Chain at Philips Electronics

Coordinating its own internal operations is a significant challenge for a multinational firm with many different subsidiaries such as Philips Electronics, let alone synchronizing the supply chain with external suppliers and customers. These large companies often look for internal improvement opportunities before venturing out with external channel partners. Philips Semiconductors, a subsidiary, decided to tackle the bullwhip effect in early 2000 by implementing a collaborative planning process with a major customer, another Philips subsidiary known as Philips Optical Services. The goal of the collaboration project was to increase sales and profit margins by enhancing customer service and reducing inventory investments through information sharing and coordinated supply chain planning. In addition to collaborative planning meetings, the project included the implementation of a software planning tool designed to support quick, effective decision making so that the two subsidiaries could react to various sources of supply chain volatility as they arose.

Philips has benefited greatly from the collaborative planning process since the implementation was completed at the end of 2001. The firm estimates that the process has resulted in a US$5 million annual reduction of inventory costs on an annual turnover of US$300 million. Annual profit also increased by approximately 1.5% from the new collaboration effort. Philips realized these benefits from increased responsiveness to changes in Philips Optical Services' market, enhanced delivery performance compared to quoted lead times, and lower levels of inventory obsolescence for products, which is essential in an industry with quickly changing technology.

Source: de Kok, Janssen, van Doremalen, van Wachem, Clerkx, and Peeters (2005).

The Importance of Supply Chain Management to Executives

It should be clear by now that managing and coordinating all the business functions that compose the supply chain among disparate locations and companies, each potentially with its own incentives, is a complex task to say the least. As a result, supply chain management must prove to generate for the company a tangible benefit to garner interest from senior-level managers and executives.

The major reason executives should take notice of innovative supply chain management practices is that supply chain management can provide a long-term competitive advantage. Even though all competitive advantages are ultimately temporary in a dynamic business environment,[16] an efficient and effective supply chain is difficult for competitors to replicate quickly because it often relies on technological integration and meaningful collaboration between channel partners. In fact, world-class supply chains embody the proverbial "holy grail" by reducing a firm's costs while simultaneously improving customer service levels by increasing the velocity and reducing the variability of goods moving through the channel.

Here are several examples of the results that supply chain improvement initiatives can generate for firms of all sizes:

- Hewlett-Packard (HP) specifically considers supply chain issues during the development of new products through a formal process called "design for supply chain" (DfSC). The cross-functional process enables employees throughout the organization to assess opportunities to reduce costs and improve customer service for all of its new and existing products across 30 product lines. From 2001 through 2006, HP realized more than US$100 million in cost savings as a result of its commitment to DfSC.[17]

- In the early 2000s Whirlpool overcame a conflicting relationship between its supply chain and its sales force and a lackluster Enterprise Resource Planning (ERP) system installation by getting back to basics and focusing on the end customers' needs. The supply chain managers also talked to Whirlpool's direct customers (small and large retailers) to gauge their service criteria and tried to build consensus throughout the other departments in the company (especially sales) for the actions that were expected to reconstruct the supply chain. In less than 2 years forecasting errors had dropped by more than 50%, and Whirlpool was delivering close to its target of 93% availability for all of its products. The company also realized direct financial benefits by reducing the working capital needed to finance finished goods inventory by 10% and lowering supply chain costs by a total of US$20 million.[18]

- The Febal Group, an Italian manufacturer of kitchen furniture with annual sales of 50 million euros, has implemented an innovative integrated production and distribution planning process that is expected to improve customer service by more than 20% and reduce delivery lead time to customers from 4 to 6 weeks to 2 to 4 weeks.[19]

- Small and medium-sized businesses can benefit from improving their supply chains as well. Malt-O-Meal (MOM) redesigned its supply chain to give the firm enough flexibility to take advantage of new distribution channels and unique customer packaging requests. MOM aligned internal functions such as demand planning and sales and inventory planning and physical distribution, and the firm reconstituted its purchasing organization to include strategic sourcing activities. MOM also invested in supply chain–enabling technology and a leadership development program to build organizational knowledge among its employees. These measures resulted in an increase in sales of 40% (fulfilled with the same amount of warehouse space used in the past), as well as a reduction in order cycle time by more than 2 days.[20]

Example 1.3. Improving Inventory Control at John Deere

Deere & Company, maker of the John Deere line of agricultural equipment, realized in 2000 that its business was too dependent on the economics of the farming industry in the United States. Consequently, its new CEO placed even greater emphasis on enhancing its other divisions that satisfy the commercial, consumer, and construction markets to diversify its customer base. In addition, he challenged every division to improve asset turnover through better management of inventory in all forms. This directive from senior management provided the rest of the company's employees with a clear challenge and reassured them that the senior management would support the initiatives that they develop to attain this goal.

Deere engaged in several different strategies to improve its asset turnover in subsequent years. The commercial and consumer divisions worked with dealers—the main retail outlets for these products—to ensure that the dealers had the right quantities of the right products at the right locations so customers could try them out on site. The dealers were skeptical of Deere's inventory-reduction plans, so Deere implemented a gradual reduction of US$250 million in inventory each year so the dealers could trust that they could operate with the lower level of inventory before reducing levels even lower. Deere also redesigned its production scheduling and planning processes to monitor the actual performance relative to the plan on a weekly basis and to make adjustments as necessary. Deere assembly lines increased the number of items they produced, as well as the frequency of production, so these items could be manufactured in quantities that matched the size of actual demand instead of in large batches. In contrast to many inventory-reduction strategies, Deere added a layer to its distribution network in the form of regional distribution centers that merge shipments from multiple factories for distribution to the dealers. These regional distribution centers were located closer to the dealers, thereby reducing the delivery lead time and allowing the dealers to carry less inventory while maintaining service levels.

Deere's inventory-reduction program has been very successful since its initialization. The total inventory investment has fallen by more than US$1 billion in the past decade, and dealer locations carry less than half of the 170 days' worth of inventory that they had in 2001. Orders now reach the dealers in 5 days or less compared to the 10 days it used to take for orders to arrive. Total assets have fallen each quarter with respect to the level of the previous year for 29 straight quarters, showing continuous improvement. The CEO estimates that the inventory-reduction program has increased the company's shareholder value added by US$120 million.

Source: Cooke (2007).

A recent survey-based study of manufacturing companies located in 23 countries dispersed throughout the world examined the connection between a firm's level of external integration with suppliers and customers and its order-winning strategies. Firms typically compete on the basis of price, quality, flexibility, or responsiveness, and the criterion that causes a customer to purchase one product over the other is the "order-winning" criterion. The study found manufacturers that compete on the basis of quality, flexibility, or responsiveness tend to exhibit higher degrees of external integration with supply chain partners; manufacturers that primarily focus on price competition do not have such a high level of external integration.[21] Competitiveness in many firms is inseparable from their supply chains' ability to come together and satisfy the needs of the end customer.

A firm's bases of competitiveness are usually established by company executives in the organization's strategic plan. All of the company's functional plans, including the supply chain plan, should be constructed to support the overall competitive strategy. For example, a procurement plan for a firm that strives to compete by producing high-quality goods should focus on obtaining high-quality materials and subcomponents from suppliers, as well as collaborating with significant suppliers to ensure timely deliveries. The supply chain plan should not emphasize sourcing the lowest-cost materials available because this does not support the company's plan to compete on quality. If the firm sought to be the low-price producer of the product, however, procuring low-cost materials would be an appropriate strategy. It is an executive's responsibility to ensure that the functional plans, including the supply chain plan, are aligned with the company's overall strategic plan. The SCOR® process reference model described previously emphasizes the importance of linking operational metrics in the supply chain with the firm's overall competitive strategy.

Supply chain management should also draw executives' attention because customers are becoming more demanding with respect to lead-time requirements, product customization, and availability.[22] As consumers order more and more products from the almost endless catalog offered by e-commerce companies, these service expectations are bound to increase in the future as well. Of course, companies can choose to satisfy this demand by holding a large amount of finished goods inventory, but that strategy is likely to prove unprofitable in the long run once inventory carrying costs (including opportunity cost of capital invested in the inventory) are considered. A responsive supply chain enables a firm to meet a variety of customer requirements with a modest level of inventory investment, securing the profitability of the operation.

Chapter Summary

This chapter has presented the underlying principles of supply chain management, the evolution of the field from its constituent business functions, and the importance of supply chain management for executives. Key takeaways from this chapter include the following:

- Supply chain management is an interorganizational approach that encompasses all of the activities necessary to produce and deliver a product to fulfill an end customer's requirements. There is a specific emphasis on a firm's collaborative relationship with suppliers and customers (such as distributors and retailers) to improve the entire system's ability to satisfy the end customer.
- Supply chain management is a relatively new concept in business, but the business functions that compose it have been performed for decades. The new focus is on the integration of these functions along with those of suppliers and customers.
- Many supply chain management efforts seek to minimize the impact of the bullwhip effect, which refers to the increasing variability of orders traveling upstream in a serial supply chain toward the manufacturer. The bullwhip effect can be largely

mitigated by realigning the incentives that companies in the supply chain face so that their own incentives induce behavior consistent with that which is best for the overall supply chain.

- Supply chain management should be an important concern for executives because it can be a source of competitive advantage, regardless of how a firm positions itself in the market. It also enables a firm to respond to the increasing demands of customers for shorter delivery times, customized products, and increased levels of availability.

CHAPTER 2

Global Supply Chain Management

Consider the supply chain for a restaurant that is committed to "local sourcing" of its ingredients for the kitchen.[1] The manager or chef must procure enough stock on a daily basis from local farms to satisfy the orders of an unknown number of customers who will dine in the restaurant on a given day and will order potentially anything on the menu. Fresh ingredients lack preservatives; therefore, they have a very short shelf life if the manager ultimately orders too much one day. Excess inventory often results in huge losses for the restaurant when the ingredients spoil. On the other hand, customers usually become very irritated if they hear that the restaurant has run out of certain dishes when they come in to dine, so the manager needs to guard against ordering too few ingredients as well.

Even if the manager were able to predict exactly how many diners would enter the restaurant on a given day and exactly what they were going to order, many things can happen to impede the restaurant's ability to satisfy the patrons' orders. The following is a list of some examples:

- A delivery truck could break down or become involved in an accident en route to the restaurant.
- The products could be damaged in transit due to poor loading into the truck or shifting within the trailer.
- The local farmer's crop could be damaged by inclement weather or pests.
- The farmer's yield could be lower than was predicted, resulting in an overall diminished level of aggregate supply. The commitment to local suppliers can limit the restaurant's ability to obtain products from other farmers located farther away.
- Ripeness of the produce could be delayed due to a lack of sufficient sunlight.

The point here is that managing a supply chain where all the suppliers are within geographic proximity to the manufacturer or service provider (in this case, the restaurant) is not without its challenges due to one major factor: variability. Variability is the nemesis of every supply chain manager because supply chain operations in practice are always executed in a world filled with unpredictability. Even if all the supply chain partners are in the same geographic area, as in Toyota's Nagoya City supply cluster in Japan,[2] or even housed within the same massive building, variability is inescapable. This variability necessarily adds to a firm's supply chain costs.

Companies can usually handle variability using two major strategies: (1) carrying extra inventory or (2) building agility and responsiveness into their supply chain operations. The former strategy is often far easier to accomplish for most companies than the latter, but it can result in high inventory carrying costs for the excess units.[3] Large quantities of inventory can also mask quality problems in a firm's production process, increasing the likelihood that substandard units will reach customers and making it difficult to identify the cause of the issues. Firms must often redesign their production or service processes if they want to achieve agility or responsiveness. Wherever possible, shifting production from a make-to-stock format to a make-to-order (or assemble-to-order) strategy will reduce inventory levels and enable the firm to be more responsive to changes in demand or in business conditions. Other strategies for increasing supply chain agility include simplifying or rationalizing the number of different product offerings, using standard parts and components in product design, and reducing the length of the supply chain.[4]

Notice that last recommendation. Reducing its length will make a firm's supply chain more responsive and able to cope with variability. This recommendation seems to run contrary to a company's establishment of a global supply chain. In actuality, it suggests that a trade-off exists between the agility (and environmental and social benefits) gained from operating locally and some yet-to-be discussed benefits of engaging the global marketplace.

This chapter begins by discussing the benefits of globalization and continues by illustrating the challenges of managing a supply chain in a global context.

Reasons for Companies to Trade Globally

Most firms in the twenty-first century have opportunities to globalize each portion of their supply chains; that is, they can engage in global sourcing of materials, global production of finished goods, global distribution of products, or all of the above. Each of these strategies can generate its own benefits for the company, some of which can be quite lucrative depending on the industry and the nature of the supply chain.

Whether the firm is acquiring raw materials, subassemblies, or finished products from international suppliers, the main benefit of global sourcing is often reduced material or product cost. Labor in developing countries is often significantly cheaper than it is in the United States or western Europe, and there are typically fewer labor restrictions to navigate as well. To illustrate the labor cost disparity between countries, consider the supply chain for T-shirts sold in the United States.[5] The cotton used to make the T-shirts is grown in the United States and shipped to China where it is spun into thread and then woven into basic, generic T-shirts. The T-shirts are then shipped back to the United States where they are printed with logos or designs before they are sold. Think about that for a second. The T-shirts, in effect, make two trips across the world before they make it to store shelves or e-commerce warehouses. The Chinese labor must be cheap enough to more than compensate for the two transoceanic shipment costs, as well as the inventory holding costs on the shirts and the raw material, or else the entire production process would remain in the United States.

Global sourcing can also provide companies with access to technology or processes that they cannot find domestically. As we will see in more detail in the next chapter, any time a firm decides to outsource a business function to another company (either domestic or international), the firm loses the institutional knowledge related to performing that function. If the trend for the entire industry has been to outsource a function, such as production, to overseas suppliers for a long period of time, it may not be possible for firms to find capable domestic suppliers. This has been the case for United States firms that sell televisions: There is no significant domestic manufacturing base for these companies to use. Even Vizio, the largest vendor of LCD televisions in the United States and a proudly American company according to its website, uses contract manufacturers in Asia to produce its televisions.[6] In other instances, it may be the case that companies in other countries have developed superior technology. This is the current situation in the alternative energy market, where European companies are largely ahead of their American counterparts on the development and large-scale implementation of these new technologies.

On the distribution end of the supply chain, firms often look to expand globally to increase market share once the domestic market becomes saturated. Internet technologies have made it easier than ever before for companies to participate in the global marketplace. In the days before the Internet, firms that wanted to sell their products in a foreign market had to set up a sales office in the market or at least engage a sales agent to market products on their behalf. Now they only need to have an Internet presence, and they can reach potential buyers all over the world. (And they can improve their ability to reach these potential buyers by smartly purchasing a few strong keywords from Google.) Individuals and modern-day cottage industries are no longer excluded from the global marketplace either, thanks to Internet intermediaries such as eBay.

Once a firm makes the decision to enter an international market, the next step is often to establish some form of manufacturing presence in the region. This could be an outsourced relationship or a company-owned factory. We will discuss the make versus buy decision in detail in the next chapter. By manufacturing close to the consumer market, the company can increase its response time and avoid most of the import duties and taxes for shipping products in from abroad. Of course, there are risks in establishing international production locations, including the need to navigate the foreign legal environment to set up a company-owned facility and the chance that outsourcing or joint-venture relationships could sour or even disintegrate in the future.

Companies are wise to consider the international production decision *simultaneously* with efforts to expand their markets internationally. If a firm wants to enter a foreign market on a permanent basis, it should at least consider establishing localized production to speed time to market and to avoid some import duties and taxes. This has been the case in Europe, where many firms have set up operations in Eastern Europe in the two decades after the fall of the Berlin Wall. China has remained a popular location for overseas manufacturing operations not simply because of its cheap labor. There are many countries in the world where labor costs are less than they are in China. Many companies are still choosing to set up new production facilities in China because this can also enable them to serve the rapidly growing Chinese consumer market quickly and effectively. Even though it may still represent a minority of the 1.4 million-person Chinese populace, the Chinese middle class constitutes a consumer market that is approaching that of the United States and Western Europe. An increasing proportion of the products manufactured in China remains in the domestic market instead of being exported.

Sources of Complexity in the Global Supply Chain

As discussed at the beginning of the chapter, even a company whose entire supply chain is located close to its facility must manage various sources of uncertainty that can negatively impact the supply chain's performance. The challenge of uncertainly only amplifies in the context of a supply chain whose operations are located around the globe. The distance and time required to ship materials and finished products between echelons in the supply chain allow for more variability to creep into the system. One way to handle this (or any amount of) variability is to carry additional inventory throughout the channel, but this remedy has the chronic problems of carrying cost and the potential masking of quality problems and their causes. A more tenable yet difficult strategy to implement is to substitute information and agility for the excess inventory. The information enables the firm to identify proactively issues due to variability that may occur in the near future and to start rectifying the problems before they even happen. The agility enables the firm's supply chain to react to the issues quickly and efficiently in a way that minimizes the negative impact felt by the customer and the firm itself. We will discuss the importance of information and agility in the global supply chain in the next section of this chapter when we consider risk management.

Another factor complicating the management of the global supply chain is the labyrinth of customs and border procedures that apply to most international shipments. Many countries levy duties on a wide range of materials and goods that are imported through their borders as a way either to earn revenue or to protect their domestic industries (or often a combination of both). Beyond the added cost of paying the import duties, though, a far bigger challenge to manage is the litany of customs and border procedures and regulations specific to each particular country. Failure to have the appropriate documentation, approvals, or licenses can cause import shipments to enter a sort of "customs purgatory" that can trap the goods for days or even weeks or months in some instances. Some of these regulations exist to increase the security of the international transportation system, but others are purely bureaucratic in nature. The risk of having a shipment of materials or finished goods delayed for a significant amount of time can ultimately undermine a firm's rationale for using a foreign supplier in the first place.

Example 2.1. Heineken's Successful Collaboration With Customs

International logistics is complicated largely by governments' ability and propensity to change their import and export laws and regulations at any time, often with little advance warning. The inability of a firm to react to these changes and comply with the new regulations can cripple its international supply chain.

Heineken, a truly global brewery with more than 100 locations in over 60 countries, learned in May 2007 from the Dutch Tax and Customs Administration (CustomsNL) that export declarations would be required for its soft drinks, which Heineken currently exported through the port of Antwerp in Belgium, as of mid-June and would be required for all of its exports by July 2009. If Heineken could not comply with the regulation, it would not be able to export through any European port other than Rotterdam, putting the company at a cost disadvantage with respect to its competitors.

Because the short lead time did not allow for Heineken to modify its ERP system to provide the declaration electronically, the company relied on its 30-year collaborative relationship with CustomsNL to devise a short-term solution. Heineken had provided CustomsNL with a high degree of transparency into its supply chain operations over the 30 years, and this had allowed for a great deal of trust to build between the two organizations. Since CustomsNL had intimate knowledge of Heineken's internal processes and control mechanisms and even had one of their own employees on the design team for Heineken's ERP excise interface, CustomsNL granted Heineken a short-term reprieve from the regulation while it augmented its system to meet the requirement in the future. The organization did not grant this kind of exemption to many other companies. The long-term relationship and history of transparency were key to ensuring the short-term continuation of Heineken's international supply chain operations without significant disruption.

Source: Baida, Rukanova, Tan, and Wigand (2007).

Fortunately for many companies, external specialists in the form of international freight forwarders and customs brokers exist to help them navigate the complicated web of customs regulations. Other experts such as export management companies and export packers provide additional specialized services to assist firms that cannot justify staffing these services internally. While the firm can obtain this expertise at less cost than it could provide internally, these specialty intermediaries represent additional relationships that must be managed in a collaborative supply chain. A few large intermediaries can provide comprehensive importing and exporting services, but many firms must use several organizations to obtain the services that they require. Each company used complicates efforts to establish a truly collaborative supply chain.

Another relatively obvious complexity of the global supply chain is the added exposure to currency exchange rate fluctuations. If a firm is purchasing supplies from or selling products to domestic supply chain partners according to a yearlong contract, it faces financial uncertainty only in the form of inflation. When the contract is with a foreign partner and in a foreign currency, however, the firm is now exposed to currency exchange rate risk, which is often much more volatile than inflation. For example, from 2005 to 2008 the Chinese yuan appreciated by approximately 18% compared with the U.S. dollar.[7] Of course, companies can always hedge against exchange rate risk by purchasing futures and options on the foreign currency that they need; the point is that international transactions necessitate that firms consider these issues when they are negotiating the purchase or the sale, and they inherently add complexity to managing the global supply chain.

For all of the discussion of the "flat world" in the past decade, thanks to Thomas Friedman's landmark best seller, many differences still exist between cultural and business norms around the world. A firm that does not research the local customs before engaging with a foreign supply chain partner stands a good chance of not realizing all of the benefits that the partnership could potentially yield. It is necessary to establish trust with the foreign business partner to share demand information and coordinate supply chain plans effectively, each of which helps to improve the performance of the entire supply chain;[8] this trust is most easily established if both parties understand the other's cultural standards and mores. This cultural education is often a nontrivial activity and must be accomplished over several years of interaction, usually including some conflicts and unsuccessful ventures along the way.

One final source of complexity in the global supply chain concerns the foreign consumer market. If a firm wants to enter a foreign consumer market, it must be sure to understand the local laws and regulations about product design, packaging and labeling, and product liability. Beyond the legal implications, however, the firm must also attempt to see the product through the eyes of the foreign consumer. This will help the firm determine the best approach to marketing the product in the foreign market, by making sure that the product fits a true need in that market. Based on market research, the firm may consider redesigning or repositioning the product in the market to make it more attractive to the new base of consumers. Undoubtedly there is some heterogeneity in the firm's domestic market that must be considered as well, but it will likely be more difficult for the firm to understand the foreign market and adapt its product and marketing approach accordingly.

Managing Global Supply Chain Risk

Organizations traditionally spend much of their time focusing on their day-to-day supply chain operations. For example, they have dedicated personnel to schedule production, monitor inventory levels, process purchase orders, and pick items to fulfill customers' orders. These operations are often beset by sources of variability such as delivery delays, shipment damages, and defective production; but researchers and practitioners have developed models, algorithms, and software packages to guide organizations to deal with the uncertainty. As a result, the financial impacts of these issues are often minimal, and they can usually be overcome with a certain amount of effort on the part of responsible personnel.

Supply chains, however, can also be affected negatively by irregular events such as natural disasters or human-precipitated events including terrorist attacks, labor unrest, or political upheaval. The occurrence of these events and the consequences if they do occur are often difficult to predict, and the situations often take place outside of the nice, neat probability structures considered by the researchers who develop operations models and algorithms.

In his landmark book *The Black Swan*, which discusses the risk of significant yet unlikely events, Nassim Nicholas Taleb describes the risk-management procedures used by the casino industry.[9] Most people would think that if any organization was an expert in handling uncertainty, it would be a casino. All of a casino's games have a foundation based on probability, and that foundation gives "the house" an edge over its players. Casinos spread the risk of losing to a "lucky" player over thousands of games and players to effectively eliminate that sort of risk as a major concern. Casinos are, on the other hand, much more concerned with being cheated by card counters and other players who try to obtain an advantage that the casino deems unfair. Consequently, all casinos have installed sophisticated security systems to identify these people and eject them from the premises if the risk becomes too large.

Taleb argues that the casino industry's risk-management system fails to consider the biggest risks of loss that casinos face. He explains that the four largest losses (or potential losses) did not stem from the lucky gamblers or the cheaters that their risk-mitigation efforts, which cost hundreds of millions of dollars to develop and implement, seek to thwart:

1. A casino lost US$100 million in revenue when a popular performer was injured in an onstage act with a tiger. No other performer could replace him in the act due to his long-term relationship working with the tiger. The casino had considered the possibility of the tiger leaping into the audience and attacking a spectator (and had insured

against it), but the possibility of the tiger attacking the performer had never been considered.

2. A contractor was hurt in the construction of a hotel addition and was so insulted by the settlement the casino offered him that he attempted to destroy the casino by detonating dynamite.

3. A casino employee who was responsible for mailing forms to the Internal Revenue Service (IRS) detailing a gambler's profit exceeding a certain amount decided to store the forms under his desk instead of mailing them. The IRS levied heavy fines on the casino.

4. A casino owner's daughter was kidnapped, and the owner decided to use casino funds to pay the ransom, which violated state gaming laws and jeopardized the casino's license.

Instead of the casino industry, Taleb recommends that organizations model their risk-management programs on those of the military. Military organizations must always be ready for *anything* that could possibly occur, whether or not anyone ever thought that it *could* occur. The casino industry, on the other hand, has dealt only with the risks that they could envision, such as the card counters. The same could be said about companies that concentrate too much on day-to-day uncertainties without considering how they would deal with the unlikely but significant supply chain disruptions that could occur at any time. Comprehensive supply chain risk-management programs must include provisions for responding to these irregular events. The company's survival could ultimately depend on it.

Recent years have seen major natural disasters cause a significant disruption of the global supply chain. The 2010 eruption of the Eyjafjallajökull volcano in Iceland caused a large portion of European airspace to be shut down, and the 2011 earthquake and resulting tsunami in Japan crippled Japanese manufacturing operations in addition to the even more significant immediate loss of life and ensuing nuclear meltdown.

One of the drawbacks of the interconnected global economy that has matured over the past two decades is the risk that local or regional events can have ripple effects far beyond the event's direct impact zone. While it may seem that natural disasters and human-precipitated events such as political upheaval in the Middle East and North Africa are happening more often, these kinds of irregular and sometimes catastrophic events have occurred throughout history. Even an article written almost 10 years ago was able to refer to a litany of events such as a typhoon in Taiwan, congestion and strikes at U.S. ports, and the SARS outbreak in Asia when highlighting the importance of managing supply chain risks.[10] The effects of these events may also be more severe for today's supply chains because many companies try to operate without much safety inventory. The supply chains of the twentieth century often had a large level of inventory throughout; this inventory could absorb variability to a large degree. As inventory levels started to drop, largely in response to the "lean revolution" started by disciples of Japanese production methods, supply chains became more vulnerable to all sources of variability. Firms that engage with global supply chain partners must ensure that they have properly identified the sources of risk and have devised appropriate action plans to respond to the threat should one arise. Better yet, these plans should try to mitigate the causes of variability occurring in the first place wherever possible.

Of course, natural disasters and human-precipitated disruptions often occur domestically as well. Scores of hurricanes have devastated various portions of the southern United States over the years and have leveled manufacturing and distribution operations in their wake. The terrorist events of September 11, 2001, disrupted much of the U.S. economy and drastically increased delivery times for shipments in the subsequent weeks. Ford Motor Company, for example, saw its output in the fourth quarter of the year drop by 13% of its production plan due to the recurrent shutdown of assembly lines that could not get parts from suppliers in Canada and Mexico.[11] The longshoremen's union strike in 2002 backed up West Coast port operations so much that some shipping containers took 6 months to reach their destinations.[12] After considering the potential impact of these disruptions, it should not come as a surprise that in the past decade many organizations have begun to engage in disaster-response planning activities as an important part of their overall supply chain planning efforts.

Another source of risk in global supply chains is the increasing likelihood of product safety concerns or consumer product fraud. Engaging international suppliers may ultimately provide a cost savings, but this savings usually comes with a loss of complete control over or oversight of the manufacturing conditions and processes. Quality problems have beset

Example 2.2. Motor Carriers' Strategic Change Following 9/11

It is not an exaggeration to say that the terrorist events of September 11, 2001, affected every business in the United States and many other companies around the world. Immediately following the events, the trucking industry faced longer delivery times, which negatively affected their customer service, and higher costs, largely as a result of higher fuel prices, more expensive insurance premiums, and increased costs of recruiting and training drivers. As a result, operating ratios for the industry as a whole increased, and approximately 11,000 motor carriers went out of business in the subsequent decade.

The impact of the events, however, depended largely on the competitive strategy that carriers employed. The carriers that pursued a cost-focused strategy performed better overall than those who focused on differentiation with high quality services. Carriers that changed their strategy from differentiation to a cost-focused strategy were also able to mitigate largely the negative effects of the unexpected events, but those that switched to another strategy or held steadfast to their current strategy were negatively affected.

These results differed from those after another disruptive event in the transportation industry: the Motor Carrier Act of 1980, which deregulated pricing in the industry. In that case, the carriers that pursued a differentiation strategy or switched to it soon after the event outperformed those that focused on cost. The difference was that the Motor Carrier Act had a larger effect on *revenues* of the carriers, while the terrorist attacks of 9/11 had a larger impact on *expenses* of the carriers. Thus a different strategy was preferable in light of the consequences of the event.

The story of the motor carrier industry in response to 9/11 presents a major lesson for firms in all industries facing the effects of unexpected disruptive events. Strategic change in response to the event is not necessary in and of itself; the appropriate response to an unexpected event is dependent upon the particular consequences of the event under consideration. Firms facing a significant event should take some time to understand the likely impact of the event and should then craft and implement a strategy that responds to it effectively.

Source: Atwater, Gopalan, Lancioni, and Hunt (2010).

well-known brands such as Mattel and Toyota in the past 5 years, and these problems have led to massive losses for the companies. It seems as though every month there is a new public warning about tainted produce such as scallions or spinach hitting the shelves in U.S. grocery stores. A few companies such as Sanlu (a milk producer) and Peanut Corporation of America have even gone bankrupt, largely as a result of intentional or unintentional product contamination or tampering. Research has estimated that the cost of one product safety or tampering incident can amount to as much as 15% of a firm's yearly revenue. As a whole, the manipulation of food quality and the counterfeiting of consumer products likely cost firms in these industries between US$10 and US$15 billion each year.[13] The results of these research studies underscore the potential negative impact of these issues and emphasize the importance of companies taking the time to prevent these events from occurring.

Many researchers have spent the past decade developing strategies for mitigating supply chain risk. It is clear that any supply chain that operates on a just-in-time basis or that simply tries to reduce inventory levels from their current point must address the issue or face the possibility of catastrophic events in the future. Risk-mitigation efforts can largely be classified into two categories: assessment and resilience.

Firms should examine their entire supply chain and try to assess the operations that are the most vulnerable to major sources of uncertainty.[14] Of course, this kind of vulnerability assessment inherently requires that the firm first understand all of the flows that compose its supply chain; this kind of self-awareness is not a trivial undertaking for many large companies with complex supply chains.[15] Once the critical operations and relationships have been identified, the firm should estimate the financial and operational impact of a disruption of these critical activities, as well as the chance that the event could occur. Monte Carlo simulation models can help quantify the financial loss and the impact of a disruption on operational metrics such as order cycle time and on-time delivery.[16]

These vulnerabilities and potential adverse events can be plotted on a risk or vulnerability map with respect to the likelihood of their occurring and their potential impact to the firm if they did occur. The map can also depict the type of vulnerability or disruption, such as a supply risk or a product-liability risk. This map helps the company visualize its risk profile to identify critical areas of exposure. The firm can then prioritize its various sources of risk based on its risk tolerance or its degree of risk aversion and can develop action plans that can be implemented once a disruption occurs.

The risk-mitigation action plans can also include proactive initiatives to reduce the impact of disruptive events in the first place. These initiatives fall under the second category of risk mitigation, which represents activities that make the supply chain more resilient, or able to react quickly to supply or demand shocks of all sizes.[17] Of course, one way to make the supply chain more resilient is to replicate production facilities around the world or to carry a large amount of inventory to absorb shocks in demand or supply. This strategy is not viable for many companies, however, because it is fraught with its own excessive costs in the majority of time periods where the supply chain is operating as the company predicts. The resilience required to handle supply chain risk can also come, instead, via flexible and agile supply chains.

Flexible and agile supply chains help companies handle all sorts of variability, whether caused by a major disruption or a day-to-day issue, such as a machine breakdown or a damaged shipment, without the need for carrying excess inventory. A recent study conducted by the Boston Consulting Group recommends eight general strategies for increasing the agility of a supply chain, which we discussed earlier in this chapter. These include

- postponing final assembly;
- standardizing products, components, and processes;
- cross-training workers;

- prioritizing customers and even creating dedicated supply chains for the most important customers;
- using demand management tools to align demand with supply;
- reducing both geographic and technological proximity of suppliers and customers.[18]

Example 2.3. Dell's and Apple's Reactions to a Supply Disruption

When an earthquake rumbled the Taiwanese city of Chi-Chi in 1999, supply flows of semiconductor chips to personal and laptop computer manufacturers stopped for a few weeks. The supplies of two of the major computer manufacturers, Dell and Apple, were affected in the same way by the disruption, but their individual customer service processes and reactions to the shortages yielded far different results.

Apple had recently unveiled several new models of computers and had taken orders for thousands of units from retailers and consumers. Since Apple had contracted for specific computer configurations with its retailers and individual customers, it could not modify the configuration when certain semiconductors were not available due to the earthquake. Apple tried to substitute a slower version of one of its models to meet the contracted orders, but the company was flooded with retailer and consumer complaints in response to this effort. Many individual consumers either switched their orders to lower-margin computers that were available immediately or canceled their orders altogether. Retailers were stuck waiting until Apple received the supplies to fulfill the original orders. Total Apple sales revenues fell in the quarter after the disruption.

In contrast, Dell's build-to-order operations model and demand management policies generated a far different result. Dell held only a few days' worth of inventory and did not have a backlog of orders for specific configurations. As a result, its customer service representatives and online sales portal could use attractive pricing to drive customer demand toward units whose parts were available.

Customers were able to receive the configurations that they ordered as if there were no supply shortage in the first place, and Dell's quarterly revenues increased by 41% year over year.

Source: Sheffi and Rice (2005).

It is also important for firms to establish a culture of risk management within their organizations so that every major decision maker naturally considers the risk implications of every decision.[19]

Study after study of risk management in supply chains mentions the need for true collaboration between supply chain partners, including the sharing of demand and supply information and the integration of information systems.[20] A company should monitor its suppliers' performance with respect to financial and operational metrics such as on-time performance, so the firm can assess the risk associated with each supplier and can make a proactive effort to reduce the likelihood of a disruption or the impact of a disruption should one occur.[21] This helps to improve and strengthen the relationship between the supply chain partners. The development of strong, collaborative supply chain relationships allows the individual firms to establish trust with each other and to realize how their ability to satisfy the final customer is ultimately interdependent. Firms with collaborative supply chain relationships are more likely to weather the impact of significant shocks to the system and emerge stronger in a postdisruption global marketplace.

An indirect benefit of creating a flexible or agile supply chain as a risk-mitigation strategy is that agile supply chains are often more efficient in their own right. It is likely that the firm will experience cost reductions *and* improved customer service performance from increasing its supply chain flexibility. This is significant because cost reductions and improved customer service measures are usually inversely related to each other; companies often have to choose to achieve one at the expense of the other. Agile supply chains can attain the elusive "holy grail" within operations management, consisting of cost reduction and improved customer service. They can also provide a firm with the flexibility to take advantage of unexpected opportunities that could arise in the marketplace just as easily as disruptions could occur. A recent study by McKinsey & Company estimated the potential impact of integrated supply chain risk-mitigation efforts as follows:

- Increase in revenue by 1–2%
- Reduction in out-of-stock instances by 10–15%
- Reduction of total supply chain cost by 5–10%
- Reduction of lead time by 10–30%
- Reduction of inventory by 20–40%[22]

Based on the results of the McKinsey & Company study, risk management not only impacts the firm in times of crisis or disruption but also can help improve the overall performance of the supply chain on a day-to-day basis.

Security Issues in International Trade

It is not an overstatement to say that the terrorist attacks of September 11, 2001, truly changed the world in which we live. In a little over an hour on that fateful Tuesday morning, international security was thrust into the world consciousness and is likely to remain there for the foreseeable future. Anyone who has boarded an airplane in the years since that day has experienced the changes firsthand. In response to the perceived threats of the day, the Transportation Security Administration has dabbled in various rules and regulations from random screenings, shoe removal, and ban on liquids to the highly publicized full-body scanners that have upset many passengers since November 2010.

With so much scrutiny being applied to each individual air traveler, it should be no surprise that the U.S. government has also implemented extensive measures to improve the security of freight shipments destined for the United States. Just as in the case of the inspection of air travelers, the government faced a challenging trade-off. Obviously, the easiest way to ensure security is to inspect every single piece of freight that enters the country. The major drawback to this, other than the enormous cost, would be that international trade in the country would effectively grind to a halt. An open-door policy toward freight imports, however, leaves too much of a possibility that illegal, illicit, or dangerous items could enter the country. Thus the government had to walk the tightrope in positioning its security policies between being too haphazard on the one hand and restricting trade too greatly on the other hand. The result has been three major initiatives that have been implemented since the September 11 attacks.[23] Any U.S. firm that engages in importing goods from abroad must understand and ensure compliance with these programs; otherwise, fines, long delivery delays, or both could result.

The Container Security Initiative (CSI) extends the reach of the U.S. Customs and Border Protection (CBP) office abroad by staging inspectors at many of the world's largest foreign seaports. These inspectors work with information that they receive about shipments in response to the so-called 24-Hour Rule that requires the transmission of cargo ship manifests for vessels bound for U.S. ports at least 24 hours *before* the cargo is even loaded onto the ship. These manifests can be transmitted electronically through the Automated Manifest System (AMS). The inspectors, along with workers from the host country, use this manifest information to label shipments as "high risk" or "low risk" before they even reach U.S. soil. High risk shipments are subject to X-ray or complete inspection upon unloading at the U.S. port. The goal in establishing the CSI was to have 80% of containers screened before they departed the foreign port in the near term with the potential of 100% screening contingent on the development of more advanced scanning equipment.

The Department of Homeland Security (DHS) wisely understood from the beginning that it did not make sense to act unilaterally in its efforts to secure the country's borders; as a result, the DHS engaged industry itself to act as a partner in security through its Customs-Trade Partnership Against Terrorism (C-TPAT) program. This voluntary initiative rewards compliant companies with a sort of "fast pass" for its import shipments through customs.[24] Interested companies must assess the security of their own supply chains and make improvements where necessary to meet the C-TPAT standards. Member companies are classified in the following three levels:

- *Tier 1* companies are new to the program. They have applied for admission into the program, but CBP has not yet validated that their processes meet the minimum security standards.
- *Tier 2* companies have processes that CBP has deemed to be satisfactory with respect to its minimum security standards.
- *Tier 3* companies have processes that CBP has judged to *exceed* its minimum security standards.

It is important to note, however, that C-TPAT status (even in tier 3) does not *guarantee* that an importer's shipments will not be held up at the border for deeper scrutiny. An importer's C-TPAT membership is only one of several factors that go into the CBP's decision to inspect a particular shipment. Officials are also concerned about the country the shipment is originating from, as well as the stated contents of the shipment. For example, a shipment being imported by a tier 3 C-TPAT company that originated in a country such as Saudi Arabia is more likely to be inspected than a shipment imported by a non-C-TPAT–member company that originated in Canada.

The CBP designed the C-TPAT program to provide strong incentives for companies to participate. According to the CBP, participating companies should expect to be subject to six times fewer inspections than nonmember companies. This makes the entire import process operate on a more predictable timeline from shipment to shipment and can reduce the amount of delay charges that the importer must pay to carriers whose equipment cannot be loaded on time. A recent poll of executives from C-TPAT–certified companies, however, has shown that these companies have not experienced a noticeable decrease in the rate of inspection of their shipments and the detention fees that they have had to pay. This suggests that C-TPAT certification may simply enable firms to achieve the status quo before the increased security measures and that those firms that do not attain the certification will be subject to even greater inspection rates and delays in the future.[25]

The final recent initiative designed to increase the security of the international supply chain is the Importer Security Filing (ISF) Message, also known as the "10+2 Rule." As of January 26, 2010, when the rule went into effect, importers (or shippers) must file 10 common pieces of information about each shipment with the CBP before the container is loaded onto a vessel bound for a U.S. port. These pieces of information include items such as the seller's name, the buyer's name, the country of origin, and the Harmonized Tariff Schedule number for the goods. The "2" in the name refers to two additional pieces of information that the carrier must supply related to the location of the goods on the vessel itself.

The ISF Message enhances the existing "24-Hour Rule" by imposing a penalty on companies that fail to comply and by requiring more detailed information about each shipment rather than simply requiring information on the manifest level. The penalty for failing to file the ISF

Message is US$5,000 per incident, and CBP officials can delay a shipment even if no fine is levied if there is a problem with the shipment's ISF Message. This delay can come in the form of an intrusive inspection of the goods or even as a message to the foreign port not to load the shipment on the U.S.-bound vessel. Some of the information required to be submitted in the ISF Message can be difficult for shippers to obtain; a survey of companies found that 58% of the respondents claimed their biggest problem in complying with the ISF Message requirements was obtaining the data in a timely manner.[26]

Other countries, such as those in the European Union as well as Mexico, are currently considering similar requirements for their import shipments. Canada is in the process of implementing a program in multiple phases that are expected to be complete in 2014.[27]

One additional way that the U.S. government and companies themselves have strengthened the security of the supply chain has been to institute traceability of the products throughout the channel.[28] Traceability refers to the supply chain's ability to track every movement of a shipment and the raw materials that compose it as far upstream as possible. Some industries, such as the airline, food, and pharmaceutical industries, have significant traceability requirements mandated by the government. Other industries can benefit from tracking their products through the supply chain should a product safety issue arise. If a particular product is found to be unsafe, the firm can use the tracking information to identify quickly the other units from the same batch or same supplier that should be recalled. Tracking technology such as RFID or GPS systems can help firms monitor their shipments en route from one level of the distribution channel to the next and can help combat product fraud or counterfeiting operations. The visibility of the products' movement throughout the system ensures that the goods are not tampered with or switched before arrival at the customer's facility.

Chapter Summary

This chapter has provided a detailed look at the global supply chain, including the reasons companies do business internationally, the reasons global supply chain management is so complex, the basic principles of risk management initiatives in the global supply chain, and the latest security measures that apply to international shipments. Key takeaways from this chapter include the following:

- Technology has made it easier for companies to find and do business with suppliers and customers located around the world. Firms must engage in the global marketplace to compete in the twenty-first century business world.
- Managing an international supply chain is much more difficult than managing a domestic supply chain because of the rules and regulations that differ between countries and the need for additional service providers to help shipments find their way to their ultimate destinations. Global supply chains also tend to be spread over a greater distance, which allows for more opportunities for variability to intervene and affect shipments.
- Building an agile or flexible supply chain can not only help a firm handle disruptions due to day-to-day variability or catastrophes but also positions the firm to be able to take advantage of positive, unforeseen opportunities to serve customers in new ways.
- Since 2001 the U.S. government has initiated three security programs—the CSI, the C-TPAT, and the ISF Message—to keep the country's borders secure while not suffocating international commerce.

CHAPTER 3

Global Sourcing

As many firms have discovered the hard way, a company's ability to satisfy its ultimate customers is largely dependent upon the performance of its suppliers. The suppliers must be able to deliver materials or provide services to meet strict delivery schedules and to attain specific levels of quality. With many firms substituting information for the need to carry inventory, suppliers play an even more critical role than they did in the past. Companies can develop a strategic advantage by nurturing strong relationships with their suppliers. While these relationships can be difficult to manage with domestic suppliers, they are even more complex and have more subtle cultural nuances if the suppliers are located abroad.

Make Versus Buy Decision

As we mentioned in chapter 1, very few, if any, companies today are vertically integrated with respect to their primary products or services. Thus they have made the decision to perform some tasks in house and to outsource other tasks to external suppliers; this is often known as the *make versus buy decision* in procurement. While it may seem like a strictly operational or at best tactical decision for the purchasing department within a company, it is actually one of the most important strategic decisions a firm can make.[1]

Whenever a firm decides to outsource an operation to another company, the buying firm gradually loses the organizational knowledge to perform that operation itself. The longer a firm goes without performing the function, the harder it is to "re-source" the function back inside the company in a way that matches the efficiency of the external supplier. This is especially true for the production of complex parts or services. To illustrate this point in class, I ask my students to integrate the function x^2 over the limits 1 and 4.[2] As undergraduate business students, I know that they have all taken a course in calculus as one of our university requirements and learned how to evaluate the definite integral that I gave them, but no one has asked them to perform this task in several years so they do not remember how to do it. The same is true for companies' outsourced operations.

To illustrate the importance of making this decision in a dynamic marketplace, consider the story of the personal computer. In the 1970s IBM was the unquestioned leader of the computer industry, but it faced a challenge from Apple and other companies that were introducing desktop computers. IBM began development of a model of its own, and it went through the make versus buy decision process as it would for any new product. This time, however, IBM made the crucial mistake of outsourcing two major components: the processor (to Intel) and the operating system (to Microsoft). As the personal computer matured, these two components became more important to consumers than the actual manufacturer of the computer itself; hence, the term "PC-compatible" was born when many competitors entered the market offering the same processor and operating system. IBM gradually lost market share until it ultimately sold off its personal computer division to Lenovo in 2005.

IBM could have been the largest technology company in the world today if it had had the foresight to retain its competency to produce its own processors and operating system.[3] Consumers would not have been clamoring for Intel processors or Microsoft Windows; they would have wanted simply an IBM personal computer above all else. Charles Fine calls this the "Intel Inside" phenomenon, where a major component supplier becomes more powerful than the original equipment manufacturer (OEM) because the consumers identify more with the component than with the good itself. Any outsourcing decision for a company bears a similar risk today. The consequences may not be quite as dire as they were for IBM's personal computer division, but the principle still applies. Apple managed to dodge this problem with its computers by maintaining in-house development of its major hardware and operating system.

This is not to say that companies should not outsource any of their components to external suppliers; they must determine smartly which competencies to retain and which can be outsourced without difficulty. A general principle is that firms should retain those activities that provide a competitive advantage and outsource the rest. This gives the focal firm the benefit of the supplier's expertise with the outsourced activities and allows the firm to invest its capital in those activities that are critical in the eyes of the customer. Fine's research related specifically to product design and manufacturing recommends that firms should try to outsource only those components for which they have the knowledge of design and production but lack production capacity. If the firm is dependent on the supplier for both capacity *and* knowledge, it runs the risk of experiencing severe supply disruptions or, even worse, having the component's status usurp that of the final product in the eyes of the consumer.

Example 3.1. Teradyne Maintains Control Over Its Outsourcing Operations

One of the risks of outsourcing a function to an outside provider is the potential that the firm can lose control over the quality and performance of the function compared to maintaining it in house. As a result, firms often retain complex manufacturing processes to ensure that they are executed to product and process specifications. Teradyne, a manufacturer of high-tech testing instruments for which precision is paramount, is one example of a company that has succeeded in outsourcing a large number of its complex production activities without losing control of its supply chain.

Teradyne took an incremental approach to contract manufacturing while ensuring that it retained control over the process. The main impetus for outsourcing was not cost reduction as it is for many firms; instead, Teradyne wanted its personnel to be able to focus on more strategic activities such as new product development and process improvement. The firm began by outsourcing production of its most basic circuit boards to a contract manufacturer in 1999. As the supplier continually produced quality output, Teradyne gradually outsourced more and more stages of its production process. Eight years later, the firm finally outsourced the final two stages, which require a great deal of testing and product customization. To maintain control of its outsourced supply chain, Teradyne kept its relationships with the suppliers that provide parts and materials to the contract manufacturers; worked with the manufacturers to build up their capabilities through training and knowledge sharing; and implemented a sophisticated information system to provide visibility to inventory levels at supplier, contract manufacturer, and distribution center levels.

The benefits Teradyne has realized from its outsourcing program have been staggering. Inventory turns more than doubled to over 5 per year in a 4-year span. Total inventory fell from US$210 million to US$80 million in this time frame. Many of Teradyne's customers are located in Asia, which is also the location of many of its contract manufacturers. Producing in the same region as the customer base has reduced transportation costs and improved Teradyne's responsiveness to its customers' demands. Customers no longer have to wait up to 16 weeks to receive an order; the average order cycle time is 8 weeks, but it can be as short as 2 weeks for rush shipments.

Source: Cooke (2008).

Total Cost of Ownership

The make versus buy decision should be evaluated on the basis of the *total* cost of using the external supplier and the *total* cost of producing the component, product, or service in house. This measure is known simply as the *total cost of ownership* (TCO), which represents all of the costs, both direct and indirect, that a company incurs by utilizing a particular source of supply. The TCO measure stands in stark contrast to many purchasing departments' method of choosing a supplier solely on the basis of quoted price. The TCO captures all of the other significant factors related to a particular supply option including the following:

- Inventory costs related to lead time and safety stock requirements
- Costs related to quality inspections and defects
- Inbound transportation costs
- Importing costs and applicable duties and taxes
- Performance and reliability quality attributes of the product or service

- Order cycle time
- Delivery frequency and reliability
- Purchasing lot size requirements
- Willingness and ability to integrate through technology such as electronic data interchange; advanced planning and scheduling systems; and Collaborative Planning, Forecasting, and Replenishment (CPFR®) systems
- Availability of supply when it is needed
- Time and effort required to manage the buyer-supplier relationship
- Trade credit terms such as offering a discount if invoices are paid within 10 or 15 days
- Financial viability of the supplier

The final criterion, the financial viability of the supplier, is especially important for vendors that supply critical, specialized components or services because the buyer may not be able to obtain supply from alternative sources should the primary vendor dissolve. If the item or service being purchased is a commodity that is readily available from many vendors in the market at the same level of performance and reliability and that does not require any collaborative or systems-integration efforts to process orders, then the financial viability of the supplier is still an important criterion in the sourcing decision but not quite as important as in the case of critical supplies.

As should be evident from the incomplete list of costs and concerns that compose the TCO, the TCO perspective is all encompassing and requires a great deal of information and modeling. Because the true computation of the entire TCO for using a particular supplier is often quite cumbersome, buyers should identify several components of the TCO that are most important for the particular item being purchased and use those to evaluate the total cost. The more critical and specialized the component is to the firm's operations and competitive position, the more criteria should be included in the TCO analysis for that component.

When the true TCO is considered in sourcing decisions, alternatives that seem to be clearly preferred on the surface can become less and less attractive. Many organizations that outsource production or services to foreign countries may not realize the degree of cost savings that they envisioned due to the relevant costs other than purchase price, including inventory requirements due to long lead times, relationship management costs, and quality problems.[4] Part of this misconception is due to the fact that relatively few firms have implemented the kinds of comprehensive cost-measurement initiatives to support true TCO analysis in global sourcing. The firm may have a lot of data related to particular costs, but it may not have a systematic way of aggregating this information to make it available to procurement personnel in a timely manner for sourcing decision making.[5]

Research into firms' procurement practices has identified a deficiency related to their holistic approach to cost measurement in sourcing. A recent study of British manufacturers and the results of their sourcing efforts in China found companies tend to perceive that the additional costs of sourcing from China, other than the purchase price of the item, are less than they actually are, thereby overestimating the benefits realized from outsourcing. Some examples of these additional costs include travel costs to establish and monitor the relationship, costs related to substandard infrastructure, cost of providing additional engineering support to the supplier, cost of dealing with cultural or language differences such as translators and gifts, cost of intellectual-property violations and consumer-product fraud, and the potential cost of negative consumer reaction to the production of goods in China. Companies must monitor these major "add-on" costs and integrate them into their supplier selection analysis to select the truly best supplier for each component or service.[6]

Another study of the sourcing criteria used by six firms in their offshore decision-making analysis found that the firms primarily focused on the quoted price, costs related to transportation and logistics services, and customs duties. The companies largely ignored inventory costs, additional administrative costs to manage the international buyer-supplier relationship, and risks that a particular business relationship could endanger the firm's future ability to import other goods or could damage the firm's reputation in the marketplace. The most common reason these companies gave for not including these additional criteria in making offshoring decisions was that the data were not readily available.[7] This study again highlights the importance of cost measurement programs to help the firm make better operational decisions overall and global sourcing decisions in particular.

One consultant recommends developing a quantitative representation of the importance and impact of each criterion in the sourcing decision; these "costs" can then be added together to evaluate a total unit cost for using each particular sourcing option.[8] The criteria can be grouped into three main categories: cost, performance, and policy. The cost factors are quantitative by nature, and performance factors such as the percentage of rejected items or the percentage of late deliveries can be quantified into a cost in a relatively straightforward manner.

The policy considerations, though, are much more difficult to evaluate in this framework. The consultant suggests that the firm estimate a (positive or negative) multiplier for the quoted unit price of the item that reflects the importance the company places on that particular policy factor. For example, if the buyer values products that are composed largely of recycled or recyclable materials, it could give suppliers using these kinds of materials a 5% or 10% reduction in their effective total unit cost, thereby making these suppliers more attractive than their competitors that do not provide this attribute. The key is to make these multipliers' values consistent across suppliers that possess the same characteristics so that the comparison of their total unit cost remains accurate.

Global Versus Local Sourcing

In the previous chapter we discussed some of the benefits of global sourcing, including reduced material cost and the access to advanced technology that may not be available domestically. In recent years, however, some companies have rethought their sourcing strategies and have "nearshored" the production of some products and services back to a market closer to the firm's home operations for a number of reasons. The justifications for this shift can be roughly grouped into two major categories: (1) the cost and risk of global sourcing and (2) the reemergence of competitive domestic manufacturers.

As Western manufacturers have flocked to China and developing countries around the world in the past few decades, the wage rates for workers in these regions, which are often cited as the main justification for outsourcing, have steadily increased. This should not be a surprise, as it is the same phenomenon that occurred in Japan, Hong Kong, and Taiwan in the 1970s and 1980s. Whenever more and more buyers flood a labor market, the cost of the labor will increase. Firms bent on utilizing the cheapest labor have had to look for suppliers elsewhere to continue their never-ending "race to the bottom."

In China, in particular, traditional coastal manufacturing hubs such as Shenzhen and Guangzhou have experienced skyrocketing wages with increases as high as 44%, exacerbated by a shortage of production labor.[9] Many Chinese laborers have chosen to return to the inland agricultural fields due to higher market prices for agricultural goods, as well as the other benefits from the *Hukou* registration system such as education and health care, which they are eligible to receive only if they remain in their rural provinces.[10] Foreign manufacturers committed to remaining in China have turned their sights to inland production possibilities to take advantage of the abundant labor that can be as much as 30% less costly than that on the coast, as well as tax incentives offered by some inland provincial governments.

Inland production, however, can be fraught with logistics challenges of its own. Central China has nowhere near the developed road and rail transportation network that exists between coastal strongholds such as Shanghai, Tianjin, Guangzhou, and Shenzhen. River transport on the Yangtze River is a significantly cheaper way to reach the coastal ports used for exporting, but the drawback is that it can take multiple days instead of, perhaps, hours. Shipments can also be delayed an unpredictable amount of time due to fluctuating water levels in the rivers. It may also be difficult to find third-party logistics (3PL) providers who can assist foreign manufacturers with distributing products within China or transporting the goods to the coast for export. Major 3PLs that say they serve inland areas will subcontract portions of the activities to local 3PLs, so foreign manufacturers would be wise to conduct due diligence to ensure that they know exactly which companies will actually be providing their logistics services, as well as each company's strengths and weaknesses.

In addition to increasing production costs, companies engaging in global sourcing also face the rising costs of ocean transportation. From 2005 to 2008, ocean freight costs more than doubled.[11] It is important to remember that international shipments may travel on the ocean for most of their voyage, but they typically reach their ultimate destination by truck or rail. The cost of these last-mile delivery services can significantly increase the shipment's total transportation cost if the prices of oil and gasoline continue their upward trajectory. For example, the cost to transport a 40-foot standard container from Shanghai to the East Coast of the United States increased from just over US$2,000 to approximately US$7,500 from 2000 to 2008. Much of this increase was due to the rising cost of last-mile delivery. If oil were to hit US$150 per barrel, it is estimated that the total cost would exceed US$10,000, and it would be approximately US$15,000 with oil at US$200 per barrel.[12] Locating production closer to the customer market base reduces the firm's exposure to variation in global transportation costs, which are largely dependent on volatile oil prices.

Working with international suppliers necessitates that firms navigate an often complex web of cultural challenges. These cultural challenges often contribute to failed alliances or partnerships between international firms.[13] Dutch social psychologist Geert Hofstede has extensively researched the facets of the differences between national cultures and between organizational cultures. He has identified five dimensions (power distance, individual versus collective, masculine versus feminine, risk averseness, and long-term versus short-term focus) on which national cultures differ. These distinct dimensions have been supported with 40 years of research and have shown to be every bit as valid in today's supposed "flat world" as they were in the Cold War years.[14]

To build a successful alliance with an international supply chain partner, firms should take the following actions:

- Even before the business relationship is negotiated for the first time, procurement personnel should do everything they can to understand the business culture in the foreign country where the potential partner operates. Understanding the culture ahead of time can better position the firm to understand its potential partner's way of thinking and can help set each party's expectations appropriately. Research has shown that unmet expectations for the relationship can be a significant source of conflict as the alliance moves forward.[15]
- Relationships should be based on mutual commitment and comparable resources contributed by both parties. If one party perceives an unequal contribution of resources between the parties to the relationship, conflict will likely result.

- The firms should jointly establish well-defined processes to manage the relationship. Each joint project should have goals, milestones, a monitoring system, and a mechanism to devise and implement improvements for the future.[16]

- The firms should have formal mechanisms for communication. Project teams with members from both firms should meet according to an established schedule, and the teams should report their progress and results to senior management of each firm. The firms should communicate results and updates about each project to their employees, perhaps through the company intranet.

- The firms should agree on the way that they will measure the savings from their collaborative efforts. This will enable a firm that is not benefiting from the relationship to go to the other and justify the need for changes to the relationship.

Just as is often the case in personal relationships, conflicts between supply chain partners can actually have some positive effects on the business relationship moving forward. Conflicts are destined to occur at some point in a supply chain relationship; if the firms can resolve the conflict successfully, this can actually strengthen the relationship and enhance the firms' commitment to each other. Of course, conflicts that are not resolved to each company's ultimate satisfaction can become a destructive force, as negative feelings can fester for years into the future.[17]

A major portion of the last chapter was devoted to discussing sources of risk in the global supply chain. Some of these risks have become so severe recently that companies have begun to shift a portion or all of their production from distant, low-cost countries to those that may have a higher nominal cost but are closer to the consumer market. Firms that seek to combat supply chain risk by building a more flexible or agile supply chain are almost required to shift finished-goods production closer to the consumer markets because offshore manufacturing is usually fraught with long lead times due to ocean transportation and customs processes. Agile supply chains that offshore finished-goods production to distant locations must either utilize expensive air freight to reduce the delivery time or carry large amounts of inventory to buffer against long lead times and delivery delays. The latter strategy, however, runs in conflict with the desire to be flexible or agile.

If firms cannot resist the allure of low manufacturing costs abroad yet still want to remain agile, they could import materials or subcomponents from foreign suppliers and then perform the final assembly domestically. This supports a build- or assemble-to-order production strategy (also known as *postponement*) that provides the firm with the ability to satisfy a wide range of customer demands without a large investment in finished-goods inventory. A recent study found that manufacturers in emerging economies are able to compete on the bases of quality, response time, and flexibility in a manner on par with their counterparts in developed economies; thus there is a strong probability that buyers can find foreign suppliers capable of supporting their postponement operations.[18] Many firms have been able to establish competitive advantages related to response time, flexibility, and inventory cost reductions from such build-to-order postponement efforts.[19]

In addition to the day-to-day operational risks of global sourcing and the risk of significant supply chain disruptions due to major events, global sourcing is also subject to risks from ethical or environmental violations on the part of suppliers. One of the consequences of the development of supply chain awareness and production offshoring has been the media and consumer expectation that domestic brands police the business practices employed by their suppliers. If a supplier operates a sweatshop or a factory that pollutes a local body of water, the court of public opinion often swings against the firm that has subcontracted with that supplier. The Gap, Nike, and Kathy Lee Gifford had high-profile brand crises in the recent past when ethics violations in various forms, including child labor, below-minimum wages, and safety issues, were found in subcontractors' facilities. A brand's reputation can be damaged greatly due to no direct acts of its own but instead as a result of doing business with noncompliant suppliers.[20]

Of course, the risk of suppliers engaging in unethical or environmentally unfriendly practices is a concern for firms utilizing domestic suppliers as well; however, the risk is greater with international suppliers for a number of reasons. Rules and regulations may be different in the foreign country than in the buyer's country. As a result, the buyer may erroneously

Example 3.2. Trust-Based Collaboration in Vietnam

Much of the press coverage of advances in supply chain management understandably focuses on large, high-profile companies boasting millions or perhaps billions of dollars in savings as a result of their supply chain initiatives; it is important to remember, however, that organizations of all sizes can benefit from managing the supply chain effectively. One such example is Metro Cash & Carry Vietnam, a German-owned grocery wholesaler that focuses on supplying the hotel, restaurant, and catering industries.

Metro has been successful in the market primarily by building long-term relationships with its suppliers and customers, allowing the firm to charge competitive prices for high-quality merchandise and customer service. Metro builds trust with its suppliers over time by offering consistent suppliers faster payment of invoices, which helps the suppliers' cash flows. While there are many potential suppliers of local produce in Vietnam, few of them are able to provide quality products throughout the year on a consistent basis. Metro's buyers talk with and visit the suppliers regularly to increase the level of trust between the two parties. Metro also commits to long-term supply contracts with its best suppliers, thereby reducing their susceptibility to market risk. Over time, this has enabled Metro to develop a strong base of reliable suppliers to ensure that it will be able to fulfill its customers' orders in a timely manner.

Metro also collaborates with its major customers, including the New World Hotel in Ho Chi Minh City. Metro entered into an alliance with the five-star hotel in 2002 in which the hotel agreed to purchase practically everything that Metro was able to supply. The hotel agreed to a regular order frequency, which has allowed Metro to optimize its transportation operations. Metro provides a dedicated account manager for the hotel and sends a staff member to accompany each shipment to the hotel and assess its quality on site. The relationship between Metro and the New World Hotel is founded on information sharing and personal relationships in a way similar to Metro's relationship with its local produce suppliers. This mutual trust has yielded financial rewards and reduced supply chain variability for each party involved— the fundamental purpose of supply chain management itself.

Source: Cadilhon and Fearne (2005).

assume that the regulations to which its operations are subject also hold for the foreign supplier. Buyers should always conduct audits of their suppliers' facilities both before an initial order and periodically throughout the relationship. The supplier's behavior can be difficult for the buyer to monitor, however, because the operations are located so far away. There are also many stories of suppliers showing buyers' auditing personnel a so-called five-star factory that is compliant and then, once the auditors leave, shifting most of the actual production to other facilities that are not compliant.[21] A good way to combat this potential problem is for the buyer to perform periodic unannounced audits or, better yet, to have its own personnel working in the supplier's facility as a permanent monitor of the operations. The strategy of "network orchestration" discussed later in this chapter can also alleviate this problem for buyers.

Just like many decisions within supply chain management, the global versus local sourcing decision must be evaluated for each particular product or component. For some products, global sourcing will be the best strategy due to its low item cost and potential access to new and innovative technologies. For others, local sourcing will be preferred due to its response time and reduction in supply variability. Some firms have adopted a dual strategy by having both local and global suppliers for their products.[22] Predictable sources of demand can be satisfied by distant global suppliers, enabling the firm to capture the low-cost purchase price. Items that have more unpredictable demand, however, are sourced from suppliers located closer to the home market to capitalize on the shorter lead time. Many buyers will use two sources of supply for the same item, procuring most of their volume from one (usually) global supplier and a smaller fraction of the volume from a closer supplier. This ensures that the firm has an alternative source of supply should the main supplier experience a delivery disruption.

Global Supplier Selection, Management, and Evaluation

It should be clear by now that a company's success in the consumer market depends on the ability of its suppliers to deliver quality products and components when and where they are needed for production of the finished good. In the past 20 years procurement has slowly risen from the status of a support activity in the business to a strategic source of competitive advantage.[23] E-procurement and other collaborative technologies have automated many of the transactions traditionally performed by a firm's purchasing department (such as processing purchase orders), and this has freed personnel to spend their time instead on strategic sourcing activities.

One of the most significant sourcing activities is selecting an appropriate supplier (or suppliers) for a particular material, component, product, or service. This supplier will provide the product or service on an ongoing basis, as opposed to simply a one-time purchase. A general supplier selection decision contains four major steps:[24]

1. Defining the specifications of the product or service to be procured
2. Establishing the exact criteria that will be used to evaluate the candidate suppliers (such as quoted price, transportation cost, payment terms, quality measures, willingness to collaborate, environmental impact, and financial stability)
3. Identifying the vendors that meet at least the minimum level of each criterion to remain under consideration as a potential supplier
4. Evaluating each remaining candidate supplier and the selection of supplier(s)

Operations researchers and decision scientists have developed analytical models utilizing various methodologies such as the Analytical Hierarchy Process, goal programming, multicriteria decision making, and balanced scorecard–type systems.[25] These models and methodologies help the decision maker to prioritize certain qualitative or quantitative criteria or both to determine the best supplier from the set of remaining candidates. Some researchers have expanded these models to include operational decisions as well, including order quantities and order frequencies.[26] A recent trend has been to incorporate environmental factors related to regulatory compliance and technologies and processes that reduce environmental impact into the supplier selection process.[27] These criteria can be incorporated directly into the decision model by adding constraints that feasible strategies must satisfy.

The decision makers in the supplier selection process should do everything they can to ensure that their analysis does not suffer from bias. Examples of bias that can enter into procurement decisions include (1) ranking potential suppliers from countries that the decision maker is familiar with higher than those from unfamiliar countries, (2) misidentifying random events as causal factors that lead the decision maker to prefer or discredit a potential supplier, (3) preferring the incumbent supplier strictly because of familiarity and a resistance to change, and (4) ignoring disconfirming evidence and only seeking to confirm preconceived notions about certain potential suppliers.[28]

To eliminate these sources of bias in the supplier selection decision, procurement personnel can engage in one or several of the following mitigation efforts:[29]

- Obtaining potential supplier ratings from personnel in related departments such as research and development, manufacturing, quality control, and distribution
- Assuming the position of a supplier's representative and trying to envision how he or she would pitch the product, negotiate the contract, and respond to the buyer's requests
- Searching for positive attributes of each potential supplier to avoid an initial preference of one over the others
- Examining the chosen supplier and looking for evidence that another candidate is actually better (as a sort of "devil's advocate")
- Making everyone involved in the supplier selection process aware of the potential sources of bias and how they can affect the decision

Once the firm has selected the supplier and begun a supply relationship, it is important to monitor and evaluate the performance of the supplier over time. Survey results showed that of 10 major elements of strategic sourcing relationship management, the most often implemented element among respondents was regular, scheduled meetings with strategic suppliers to discuss past performance and strategies for improving future performance.[30] These review meetings are essential ways to address problems in a buyer-supplier relationship, and they can help address conflicts within the relationship head on without letting them reach a point that they cause irreparable damage to the arrangement. Supplier evaluation is one part of the communication link between buyers and suppliers that contributes to a mutually beneficial supply chain relationship.[31]

Example 3.3. Strategic Sourcing at Ann Taylor

Many organizations have implemented strategic sourcing processes with their primary component suppliers, but they may have overlooked the benefits of developing similar strategies for their indirect procurement activities. This was the case at Ann Taylor, a large retailer of women's apparel with annual sales eclipsing US$2 billion in 2006. Ann Taylor had decentralized responsibility for its indirect procurement products and services into its functional areas such as construction and marketing. Each of these departments was responsible for specifying procurement requirements, selecting suppliers, negotiating contracts with suppliers, placing orders against the contracts, and evaluating suppliers. Centralizing the sourcing of these products and services instead would allow Ann Taylor to leverage its company-wide purchasing power with a few common suppliers to secure preferential pricing and higher levels of customer service.

The firm's new senior vice president (SVP) of logistics sought to capitalize on the firm's recent strategic sourcing initiatives for store supplies by expanding the effort into the entire portfolio of indirect materials and services. This expanded centralized strategic sourcing program faced resistance from the functional areas, however, because the functions were worried about supply disruptions related to allocating the responsibility to a central office. At the same time, other members of the senior management were reluctant to fund these activities because they were skeptical of earning the firm's requisite return on the investment from the project.

The SVP of logistics and his team were able to implement the project and realize average indirect procurement cost savings of 16% by developing a series of steps to gradually build support for the initiative from the internal skeptics. They started the project slowly by focusing on items the functional employees would not be too concerned about if the supply was disrupted. They also measured the financial impact of the initiatives and documented the current savings before adding products and services to the program. This meticulous bookkeeping was necessary to prove that the program was self-funding, and it gradually gained the executives' support as a result. Open and frequent communication of the results of the program throughout the company and with major suppliers was also essential in garnering support.

Source: Romano and Finley (2006).

Innovative Supply Management Relationships

With the establishment of a supply chain orientation over the past few decades and the ability to outsource functions that were traditionally performed in house, many firms have begun working more closely with their suppliers than ever before. As a result, several innovative supply management relationships have evolved, further improving the supply chain as a whole. In this section we discuss three such relationships and initiatives that have been very beneficial.

Network Orchestrators

The supply chains for many of the products we use every day are much more complicated than they might first appear. Computers, televisions, smart phones, e-readers (such as the one you may be using to read this book), and other items that have become essential for life in the twenty-first century are composed of hundreds and possibly thousands of parts, each of which potentially comes from a different supplier in a different country.[32]

What you may have never considered is the level of coordination required to ensure that every part is available when and where it is needed to manufacture the final product. Managing and synchronizing the efforts of all of those disparate suppliers can often be overwhelming. Just ask Boeing. Its 787 Dreamliner was scheduled for delivery to its first customer in September 2011, a full 3 years later than expected, largely because of Boeing's difficulty in coordinating its composite global supply chain to deliver on time for final assembly. It is estimated that Boeing has lost billions of dollars due to the delay, in the form of lost revenue, diminished brand reputation, concessions to airline customers who have had to wait for delivery, and payments to suppliers whose production schedules were negatively affected by the delay.[33]

For companies that want to leave the coordination of their suppliers and even their production to an outside company, firms known as *network orchestrators* may be the solution. A network orchestrator takes a product that a customer wants to build and then uses its proprietary network of suppliers and their known capabilities to develop an optimal supply chain specifically for that particular product.

The most famous network orchestrator is a Hong Kong–based company called Li & Fung, which was established in 1906. Li & Fung specializes in apparel products, but the firm has also expanded into other consumer products. Over 100 years of experience working with Asian manufacturers has given Li & Fung a proprietary knowledge of each individual manufacturer's operations and capabilities, as well as a strong relationship that can induce manufacturers to perform whatever function Li & Fung requires of them for a particular product. Li & Fung uses this network of suppliers to assign each step in the supply and production processes for the final product to the supplier best positioned to satisfy the requirement on time and at a competitive cost. They can even assign half an order to one manufacturer and half to another manufacturer if Li & Fung has confidence that both will produce according to the specification so the customer cannot tell that the order was produced in two different places.

The intimate network of more than 8,000 contract manufacturers and suppliers is Li & Fung's major asset. Competitors may try to mimic the network, but it will be difficult to develop such deep relationships with suppliers as Li & Fung has cultivated over the past century. The suppliers are willing to accommodate Li & Fung's special requests in a way that they would not for companies with which they do not have such a strong relationship. Relying on this broad, diverse network of suppliers is the only way Li & Fung can effectively create a supply chain from scratch for each order it receives. This relationship network will ensure Li & Fung's success in the endless sea of start-up online marketplaces and middlemen.

Supplier Development Programs

Many buyers that have recognized the importance of their suppliers to the overall performance of the supply chain have implemented supplier development programs to help suppliers improve their operations and performance. In most supply networks, the OEM is the largest entity with the most resources. Since most of the suppliers are quite small compared to the OEM, they cannot necessarily invest resources to improve their operations at the level that the OEM could. If the larger buyer wants the relationship to continue into the future, it is incumbent upon the larger entity in the supply chain to invest some resources to help the supplier achieve the level of performance required by the buyer.[34] Otherwise, the buyer will be forced to look for new suppliers continuously without ever establishing a long-term relationship and without realizing the benefits that can result.

Even though some organizations today would still characterize their relationships with their suppliers as adversarial, the practice of sharing resources with key suppliers has been around for a long time. In 1993 a survey found that over 60% of the companies surveyed had a formal supplier development program, and over 90% of these programs had been in place for more than 1 year at the time of the survey. The main rationale reported for the establishment of these programs was to improve the quality, on-time delivery, customer service, and cost that the buyer received from its suppliers.[35]

Supplier development programs can take many forms, but they all involve a buyer investing its resources either directly or indirectly in the supplier. Indirect supplier development programs consist of activities such as supplier evaluation and incentives where the buyer limits its investment in the supplier; in these cases, the supplier still must have the impetus to initiate improvement. Direct supplier development programs, however, involve the buyer investing tangible human or capital resources to assist the supplier.[36] This direct investment can include placing engineering or quality control personnel in the supplier's facility to aid improvement initiatives, inviting suppliers' representatives to the buyer's facility to share knowledge about processes and engage in other educational programs, and even loaning funds to finance the supplier's purchase of materials or capital investments to support the buyer's requirements.[37] Studies have shown that this investment can increase a supplier's satisfaction with and commitment to a relationship with a buyer.[38]

Collaborative Supplier Relationships

As the notion of the supply chain developed, firms realized the benefits they could obtain by collaborating with their major suppliers and customers. Some of these benefits were reduced inventory and transaction cost, improved forecasting and planning, and higher levels of customer service.[39] Over time, standard collaboration arrangements evolved in the market, each with the goal of benefiting each member of the supply chain in its own unique way. In this section we briefly discuss several of these collaborative relationships.

The apparel industry has been notorious for having long lead times, which were estimated in the 1980s to be 66 weeks from design to delivery to retailers' shelves.[40] The length of the supply chain forced the apparel makers to plan production based on forecasts of what demand would be over a year in the future. Predicting demand that far into the future is a difficult proposition, and not surprisingly, the forecasts in the industry suffered from high levels of inaccuracy. This increased the likelihood that apparel makers would not have enough supply of the items that proved to be popular and way too much stock of the items that did not sell well. Since the selling season for fashion apparel was at best 3 or 4 months long, the long production chain lead time prohibited the firms from executing additional production runs for the popular items.

With the help of consulting firm Kurt Salmon Associates, U.S. apparel manufacturers developed and implemented a set of processes that came to be known as *quick response* (QR). Information sharing between the partners in the supply chain through advanced information systems such as point-of-sale (POS) and electronic data interchange (EDI) systems formed the backbone of QR programs. Collecting and transmitting POS data using bar codes and universal product code (UPC) labels helped to mitigate the bullwhip effect by providing vendors with visibility into the actual demand realized at the retail level. The sharing of other information such as purchase orders, invoices, advanced shipping information, and order status reports via EDI also helped to reduce the overall lead time in the apparel supply chain. Subsequent stages of implementation included advanced distribution processes such as cross-docking and container tracking, as well as collaborative planning between the supply chain partners.

A successful QR implementation can have a significant impact on all of the firms in the supply chain in the form of increased customer service, faster delivery times, higher inventory turnover, increased revenue, and fewer markdowns. The success of QR programs in the apparel industry has led firms in other industries to apply similar principles and processes to their supply chains where they fit. The grocery industry, in particular, adopted its own form of QR in the early 1990s, known in the industry as *Efficient Consumer Response* (ECR).

Advanced levels of QR implementation require the retailers to allocate their inventory replenishment decisions or even their stocking decisions to the vendors. This facet of QR has been adopted in many other industries as well in the form of *vendor-managed inventory* (VMI) and *category management* (CM) programs.

In a VMI relationship, the buyer charges the supplier with determining appropriate inventory levels and scheduling replenishment shipments at its facilities.[41] These types of arrangements can occur between a retailer and a vendor, as well as between a manufacturer and a component supplier. The supplier in a VMI relationship has real-time access to inventory levels at the buyer's facilities so that the supplier can monitor sales and determine when replenishments are required to meet the buyer's preestablished inventory availability and turnover targets.

Both the buyer and the supplier can benefit greatly from a successful VMI program. The buyer does not experience inventory monitoring and ordering costs that it would by managing the inventory itself, and the real-time monitoring by the supplier results in higher levels of product availability and customer service. The supplier has better visibility into the actual demand at the customer level, which reduces the demand variability generated by the bullwhip effect in a traditional serial supply chain. The supplier is able to incorporate accurately timed customer requirements into its production and distribution planning processes to realize added efficiencies.

A CM program takes the collaboration that exists in a VMI relationship to a higher level. The buyer, a retailer in this case, allocates not only the inventory replenishment decisions to the vendor but also the product assortment decisions. Thus the vendor determines which products should be stocked in a given area of retailer shelf space. The retailer can even assign a so-called *category captain* to be in charge of an entire consumer product area. For example, a retailer could make Coca-Cola the category captain for soft drinks at its stores; Coca-Cola would then determine the amount of shelf space to assign to each of its products, as well as to products sold by PepsiCo and other smaller soft drink companies. CM practices have been estimated to increase revenues by as much as 16% for retailers and 8% for manufacturers.[42]

Retailers that assign product assortment responsibilities to their vendors often do so because the vendors are seen as the experts in the product segment. A retailer cannot be an expert on the demand and marketing characteristics for every product it sells; thus Coca-Cola should have even more insight about the soft drink market than Walmart or Kroger has. The retailers also avoid the managerial costs of performing assortment analysis for each product segment on their own.[43]

On the vendor side, the opportunity to be a category captain requires a great deal of resources to perform the assortment analysis. In return, the captain has the chance to tip the scales in favor of assigning its own products slightly more shelf space than competitors' products when the data suggest an even allocation, in addition to cementing a strong relationship between the retailer and the captain vendor for the future. While some studies have shown that category captains do not take advantage of their position to assign a disproportionately large amount of shelf space to their products to the detriment of major competitors,[44] there have been some examples where noncaptain brands have been excluded from the market or at least severely limited. This has led antitrust advocates to criticize and question the practice in the media. To prevent captains from overstocking their own products and restricting competition, retailers should ensure that noncaptain companies provide their input to the captain's recommendations and adjust the final allocation accordingly.[45]

Another type of collaborative relationship that has improved the performance of many varied supply chains is CPFR®. CPFR® is a nine-step business process developed and maintained by the Voluntary Interindustry Commerce Standards Association to provide manufacturers, suppliers, and retailers with a framework to share critical supply chain information and develop collaborative consensus forecasts and production and delivery schedules. Just as with other collaborative relationships, the goal of CPFR® is to improve customer service throughout the supply chain while reducing inventory levels and their associated costs.

Many supply chains over the past two decades have benefited from CPFR® initiatives. One such example is the retailer Sears and its Michelin tire vendor. After a year of engaging in a CPFR® program with automated data sharing and monthly meetings, in-stock levels at Sears stores and distribution centers increased by 4.3% and 10.7%, respectively. At the same time, combined inventory levels for the two firms decreased by a total of 25%. Both Sears and Michelin also experienced indirect benefits such as a more structured method for handling exceptions that inevitably arise in the supply chain and improved business processes due to the need for both firms to map their processes during the implementation of the CPFR® program.[46]

Chapter Summary

This chapter has examined important considerations that firms must address when developing a global sourcing strategy including the make versus buy decision, global versus local sourcing, and the supplier selection and evaluation process. The chapter closed with a discussion of several innovative supplier relationship structures that have improved the ability of supply chains around the world to satisfy their end customers' requirements in an efficient manner. Key takeaways from this chapter include the following:

- One of the most important strategic decisions a firm can make is its choice of which competencies to keep in house and which to outsource to external suppliers. Outsourcing for knowledge of how to perform the activity in addition to simply the need for capacity can put the firm in a precarious position at the hands of a potentially powerful supplier.
- The company should evaluate its potential suppliers on the basis of the TCO instead of simply on the quoted price of the

item. Additional costs associated with different suppliers can make a particular supplier with a higher quoted price a better choice in the long run than a supplier with a lower quoted price.

- Utilizing global suppliers almost always increases the lead time and the variability in a firm's supply. Firms must analyze whether the lower cost of a foreign supplier compared to a local option outweighs the risks that come with having such a distant supplier.
- Collaborative relationships such as QR, VMI, CM, and CPFR® can improve customer service levels while simultaneously reducing supply chain inventory through the use of advanced information technology and information sharing.

CHAPTER 4

Global Transportation and Distribution

Contrary to what some media pundits may think, the United States does, in fact, export billions of dollars' worth of goods and services each year. Organizations that want to establish markets abroad for their products and services face as many challenges as those that wish to purchase materials and components from foreign suppliers. Some of these challenges are similar to those of global sourcing, including long lead times, exchange-rate risk, cultural differences, and labyrinthine customs and border procedures. Some, on the other hand, are unique to international distribution, such as designing and marketing products for foreign markets and distributing products in regions with substandard infrastructure. This chapter will discuss the important considerations and current best practices to help firms make their venture into the global marketplace a successful one.

Structuring International Operations

Once a firm begins to consider an entry into a foreign market, it must develop a strategy for how it will structure its foreign operations. There are three major facets to the strategy:

1. Product customization
2. Ownership structure of foreign operations
3. Hierarchy of management in foreign operations

When entering a foreign market for the first time, a firm can either market the same product that it currently sells domestically, or it can customize the product to suit the preferences of consumers in the foreign market. Recognizing the distinct cultural and social differences that exist between people in different countries, as well as the different levels of availability of materials that can be used for local production, it should be no surprise that there are very few products that are truly the same regardless of where they are sold in the world. An example is snack food such as Snickers and M&M candies, Oreo and Chips Ahoy cookies, and Lay's potato chips. Even these can differ somewhat, however, in that different flavors are often offered in addition to the original product. I have feasted on green tea-flavored Oreos, lychee-flavored potato chips, and coffee-flavored gum in China and masala-flavored potato chips in India. All of the original flavors were available on the shelves as well. Another example of a global product is liquor, especially blended and single-malt Scotch whisky that has recently become a sign of wealth and sophistication in countries outside the United States and Western Europe.

Computer accessories are another type of product that is largely global. Thanks to standardization in connection that comes from designing these items to utilize the USB ports on computers, products such as memory sticks and cards, printers, and laser pointers can remain relatively unchanged wherever they are sold in the world.

Other items are drastically different from one country to another. Computers themselves have keyboards that accommodate additional characters required by different languages.[1] Automobiles in Europe tend to be smaller and more futuristic looking than they are in the United States. They are designed to fit the narrow streets and to have the fuel efficiency required to deal with gasoline prices that can be as much as US$6 to US$9 per gallon. Even fast food restaurants such as McDonald's and KFC pair locally inspired items alongside their staples such as the Big Mac or Original Recipe Chicken.

The second strategic decision facing firms deciding to enter a foreign market is the ownership structure of the effort.[2] Firms can either set up a specific entity, contract with a local entity in the foreign country, or manage the process entirely from abroad. The structural options differ in the degree of control that the home office is able to maintain, as well as the risk of asset loss due to an unsuccessful venture. The options available to most companies can be categorized into the following set, which are listed in order of increasing risk of investment loss:

- *Exporting.* The easiest way for firms to enter a foreign market is simply to take product orders from foreign customers and export the goods from their domestic locations to fulfill the orders. The company could identify new customers by establishing a foreign sales office located in the new market, by working with an intermediary who will market the product in the new market, or by purchasing Internet search keywords or placing banner ads to attract potential customers to the firm's website. The Internet has fundamentally changed the global marketplace by opening foreign markets to small businesses and even individuals.[3] An exporting strategy results in minimal risk of loss for the company, but working with an intermediary can require that the firm relinquish control over how the product is marketed in the foreign marketplace. The transportation costs are also high in exporting because items must travel from domestic supply locations to the foreign market. Exporting is often a preferred strategy for those companies that want to test their product's appeal in a foreign market without making any significant, long-term commitment.

- *Licensing.* In a licensing agreement, a firm—the *licensor*— transfers some form of intellectual property to a foreign company—the *licensee*—in return for a royalty fee each time the property is used. Licensing arrangements are common in manufacturing where the licensor permits the licensee to use proprietary processes or materials that the licensor developed. This relationship can allow the licensor to reap the benefits of its intellectual property in the global marketplace without requiring a large start-up investment. The risk, however, is that some countries' legal systems do not protect intellectual property as strongly as the United States and Western Europe do; as a result, piracy and copyright infringement activities can eat into the licensor's revenues.[4]

- *Franchising.* Franchising is a kind of licensing arrangement where the licensor packages many different forms of intellectual property such as brand reputation, operational processes, supplier relationships, and marketing and promotion activities together for the licensee in return for a large royalty payment in the form of a percentage of sales. Franchising is most appropriate for companies whose operations require minimal specialized skills to expand their global presence quickly. Such

industries include fast food and other restaurants, pet care, and
hotels.

- *Joint venture.* Under a joint venture agreement, the firm starts
  up a new company with a foreign partner. The new firm is
  based in the foreign country and is owned jointly by the two
  principal partners. The ownership split is often 50-50 or 51-49
  between the two partners, but other combinations are possible. The focal firm, the one initiating the agreement with
  the foreign partner, is actively investing in the foreign country,
  so there is increased risk of loss from this strategy compared
  to exporting or licensing. In return, however, the focal firm
  seeks to retain more control over the operation than it would
  have with one of the aforementioned strategies, and it also can
  obtain access to the foreign company's local management and
  market expertise, as well as its established distribution network.

  Joint ventures may also be the preferred strategy to cope
  with actions and policies instituted by the foreign government.
  In some cases, the government may restrict foreign ownership
  of facilities and operations in its country, requiring foreign
  firms to partner with a local firm in a joint venture. India, for
  example, does not allow foreign retailers to establish operations that compete directly with Indian retailers. As a result,
  Walmart formed a joint venture with Bharti Enterprises (based
  in New Delhi) and opened its first wholesale facility in May
  2009. British retailer Tesco has a similar joint venture arrangement with the Tata Group, one of India's largest companies.[5]
  Many countries, however, have relaxed these restrictions on
  foreign investment in recent years to attract new attention
  from abroad. Joint ventures can also protect a foreign firm
  from the risk of having its operations nationalized, or taken
  over by the government. Nationalization of foreign operations
  was more of a risk in the mid-twentieth century, but it can still
  be a concern today, especially in countries with dictatorial or
  totalitarian governments.
- *Subsidiary.* A firm can retain maximum control over its foreign
  operations by setting up a wholly owned foreign subsidiary. Of

course, this strategy also exposes the firm to the greatest risk of investment loss, since there is no foreign partner with whom to share the investment. The firm may be able to benefit from the elimination of customs duties and other import taxes based on the specific country's policies because the subsidiary can be treated as a domestic firm within that market. There may be regulations, however, that limit the amount of profit that can be taken out of the foreign country and used by the parent company elsewhere.

Example 4.1. Motorola's Failed Joint Ventures in China

Perhaps no company illustrates the risks of setting up joint ventures in international markets more than Motorola does. When Deng Xiaoping opened China to Western investment in the late 1970s, Motorola was one of the only companies to jump at the opportunity. The Chinese government told Motorola it could manufacture and sell products in China if it was willing to take on a Chinese company as a joint venture partner and share its proprietary technology with the Chinese firm. Motorola was able to negotiate this clause out of the arrangement initially, but by the time it was the largest foreign company operating in China in 2001, Motorola had two Chinese partners, 170 Chinese suppliers, and 18 research and development centers in China.

Over time, Motorola suffered from the loss of its workers and technology to Chinese suppliers and partners. The technology was slower to migrate to the partners, and Motorola executives to this day claim that they never actively shared technology with them. The bigger problem was the defection of its workers to the Chinese firms. Motorola would train Chinese workers who would work for a year and then leave to work for a Chinese competitor. Noncompete clauses that are standard practice in Western business were not enforceable in China at the time. The fact that Motorola had so much of its research and development in China, at the behest of the Chinese government, further exacerbated the drain on the company's intellectual capital when these engineers left for jobs with competitors.

Once the largest foreign company and the clear market leader for cellular phones in China, Motorola's market share had dropped to 20% in 2006 and was only 2% in 2010. A major factor in its demise in China and globally was the unfortunate role Motorola ultimately assumed in the education and training of a large number of its competitors' employees.

Source: Kilzer (2011).

The parent company must also decide how to manage and oversee its foreign operations. The firm can either take a hierarchical approach where all major decisions are made by the home office, or it can allow the foreign operations to make certain decisions on their own, thereby adopting a somewhat decentralized management structure. A hierarchical system is the best way for the parent firm to ensure that all of its operations adhere to its common global strategy and to facilitate the sharing of best practices between the global operations. This hierarchy can also enable the firm to realize economies of scale by centralizing certain firm-wide operations in one parent location to capitalize on the total firm volume requirements for the activity. A decentralized structure, on the other hand, allows the firm to capitalize on its local management's expertise in motivating and evaluating workers in its own culture. Of course, a hybrid structure is also possible where the parent firm allocates the authority to make certain decisions to the local management but also holds onto major strategic decisions in the home office.

Global Transportation Management

Firms have five major options to choose from when they want to transport goods from one place to another: road, rail, water, air, and pipeline. These methods are commonly known as the *modes* of transportation. In this section we discuss each of these modes in detail and highlight some of the current issues of which companies should be aware. We also describe several intermediaries that can assist firms with various parts of the international transportation and documentation process if they do not want to handle these activities in house.

Before we discuss the modes in particular, it is important to say something about transportation rates in general. Some rates are based solely on the size of the equipment that is being moved (such as in truckload or container shipping), and other rates are based on particular characteristics of the freight including density, susceptibility to damage, stowability, weight, and handling requirements (such as in consolidated forms of transportation). All rates, however, are subject to the general imbalance of trade flows between regions. Like most other products or services, transportation rates are based on supply and demand. It is much more expensive to send a shipment from China to the West Coast of the United States than it is to send the same goods in the opposite direction.[6] Carriers give a large discount for shipments traveling opposite the main trade route so that their containers, vessels, or trailers do not have to travel back to their origin point empty.

Road

Road transportation, usually in the form of trucking, is the most popular mode of transportation around the world. Trucking accounts for over 80% of the total spending on freight costs in the United States, and there are more than 600,000 registered motor carriers in the country.[7] In smaller countries such as the United Kingdom, trucking can move over 80% of the gross freight tonnage because most of the shipments travel relatively short distances.[8] Trucking's main advantage over other modes is its accessibility and versatility. Most companies around the world can receive a delivery from a truck of some size, but relatively few firms have their own aircraft landing strip or ocean crane on site.[9] Many trucks are even equipped with liftgates, which are platforms that can be raised and lowered at the touch of a button to allow delivery of heavy shipments to customer locations that do not have a receiving dock. Different types of trucking companies specialize in certain sizes of freight, from those that handle small packages (parcel carriers) to those that transport a few pallets (less than truckload) or many pallets (truckload).

Regardless of where a shipment originates and what goods it contains, there is a strong possibility that the goods will be transported by a truck at least at some point in its journey. Shipments that travel long distances via either water or rail carriers rely on trucking carriers to provide the initial pickup from the shipper and the final delivery to the customer (known as the *consignee*). The use of more than one mode of transportation to deliver a single shipment is an *intermodal* operation. Some popular intermodal combinations are ocean-truck, ocean-rail-truck, air-truck, and rail-truck. Some trucking companies even work with rail carriers to transport their trailers on flatbed railcars over long distances in the western United States to reduce the need for drivers as well as the travel time.

International agreements such as the North American Free Trade Agreement (NAFTA) and the European Union (EU) have facilitated the movement of cross-border shipments. In fact, the EU's common market has made shipments between countries mimic the movement of shipments between states in the United States.[10] One of the major components of the NAFTA agreement between Canada, the United States, and Mexico addressed trucking by specifying that each country's trucking carriers would be allowed to move freely within the others' borders to deliver shipments. This was the case for Canadian trucks in the United States shortly after the passage of the NAFTA agreement in 1994, but it was not until 2011 that the same became true for Mexican trucks.[11]

All modes of transportation have been beset with rising fuel costs for the last decade, and trucking is no different. While carriers have passed along some of this cost increase to their customers in the form of higher rates or fuel surcharges, the carriers have certainly borne a share of the rising prices. Expecting that higher costs are here to stay, many carriers have begun replacing their existing tractors with more fuel-efficient or aerodynamic models. Freightliner, one of the leading manufacturers of freight tractors, has designed tractors with aerodynamic features that can result in an annual fuel savings of up to US$2,750 per truck. Carriers have also implemented maximum speed limits for their drivers as well as devices to prevent them from idling their trucks, both of which further reduce fuel consumption.[12] These policies have the added benefit of reducing the environmental harm caused by freight transportation, which has the largest negative environmental impact of all the processes in the logistics system.[13]

The entire motor carrier industry has been facing a shortage of capacity for years. Part of this capacity shortage is due to the difficulty in finding qualified drivers. Many truck drivers could also choose to work in the construction industry during periods of expansion in real estate development. This was the case in the mid-2000s, and carriers had to invest their profits at that time to increase driver benefits and driver retention. Many of the current drivers are over the age of 55, which means that they will need to be replaced in 10 to 15 years when they retire; there is concern that there are not enough young drivers to fulfill this need.[14] New hours-of-service laws for U.S. truck drivers established in 2004 and contested in court until July 2011 have improved conditions for drivers by increasing their amount of required off-duty time, but it is expected that carriers will further lose capacity due to this reduction in drivers' available hours.[15]

As of 2008, licensed drivers were not eschewing the trucking industry for work in construction, yet the trucking industry as a whole still does not have enough capacity to meet the overall demand. This is largely due to the fact that over 3,000 U.S. trucking companies went out of business between 2008 and 2011, which represents a loss of approximately 13% of the total industry capacity. Analysts anticipate a shortage of 180,000 trucks by the end of 2012, which is exacerbated by a current shortage of manufacturing capacity and working capital on the part of truck manufacturers.[16]

The European trucking industry is experiencing similar capacity shortages for a number of reasons. There has been a recent shift of freight traffic to the road and away from other modes. Trucks encounter increased congestion on the dense European road network due to increased automobile traffic as well. European governments have also passed legislation that has hampered carriers' efficiency, including new hours-of-service laws for drivers that are even stricter than those in the United States and limiting freight traffic in urban areas to smaller vehicles and to daytime deliveries only (to reduce noise pollution while people are sleeping).[17]

Shippers can mitigate the rising costs of transportation and reduce the environmental impact of their distribution systems by optimizing their transportation networks. Many researchers and third-party logistics providers have developed complex models and algorithms to improve the consolidation of shipments and the utilization of transportation equipment to meet certain service levels and delivery windows. Some of these models also seek to integrate inventory or production decisions along with the transportation decisions to develop a minimum total cost solution.[18] There are several general strategies, however, that firms can use to improve their overall transportation efficiency without building complex analytical models:

- Provide visibility across all global locations and shipments to the freight management function so that the firm can identify all possible consolidation opportunities.[19]
- Collaborate with other shippers potentially outside the firm's supply chain to find additional consolidation opportunities.
- Work with carriers to utilize their expertise in improving transportation efficiencies.
- Remember to include inbound freight shipments as part of the total transportation management process to discover new efficiencies.
- Describe the rationale behind improvement efforts in terms that clearly relate to logistics processes and activities such as "reducing transportation miles" instead of a metric that is further removed from personnel's frame of reference such as "reducing carbon dioxide emissions."[20]
- Establish VMI or other automated replenishment programs with major customers so that the firm can adjust shipments and deliveries to match other customers' requirements and utilize transportation equipment more effectively.[21]
- Utilize standard pallet sizes that conform to the common dimensions of trailers wherever possible, so that a higher percentage of the available space in the trailer can be utilized.[22]

Example 4.2. Kimberly-Clark's Shared Distribution Channel in Europe

In 2003 Kimberly-Clark conducted a trial distribution arrangement with Lever Fabergé to share transportation capacity for common customers in the Netherlands. In the first incarnation of the strategy, each firm utilized one-half of a truck to create full truckload shipments to the customer. This collaborative distribution strategy has since become much more commonplace throughout Europe.

This shared distribution strategy has many benefits for all parties involved in the relationship. Trucking costs in general are cheaper on a per-unit or per-pound basis for full truckloads as opposed to smaller shipments. By sharing capacity with other shippers, vendors are able to realize these lower transportation costs while still making smaller, more frequent shipments to their retailers in response to their requests. The retailers receiving these consolidated shipments were requesting smaller, more frequent shipments from the vendors so they could have inventory levels that more closely mimic their customers' demand patterns over several days' time. If the retailers had to handle full truckloads, they would have enough units in inventory to last them potentially weeks or months, leading to high inventory carrying costs and low asset turnover. The shared distribution strategy enabled the vendors to meet their customers' demands in an economical way. The collaboration also improved the efficiency of carriers by ensuring that more trucks on the road were loaded full of freight as opposed to half-empty trucks wasting fuel and generating excess pollution.

It is important to note that these shared distribution strategies are fulfilling the traditional role of wholesalers and distributors in the supply chain without the need to capture additional profit margin. These traditional organizations add value by making products supplied by many different vendors available to retailers in a single, large shipment instead of requiring that they order from each vendor individually. Shared distribution requires inventory visibility for all vendors at the retail level, as well as a great deal of trust among all parties involved; thus its application is limited to major vendors and major retailers. It is likely, though, that this collaborative distribution will become even more popular, which should make the competitive environment even more difficult for many wholesalers and distributors.

Source: Cooke (2011).

Rail

The railroad industry in the United States has experienced a renaissance of sorts over the past few decades. While rail was the dominant mode of transportation in the country at the turn of the previous century, rail carriers gradually lost ground in the market to motor carriers; by the 1960s and 1970s, rail was used primarily to move heavy, bulk goods over long distances. The industry consolidated to the point that now there are only seven class 1 railroads in the United States; the rest are local or switching railroads that operate exclusively within a port area. The renaissance began in the 1970s with the passage of deregulation legislation and the development of intermodal operations. Rail carriers now play a major role in transporting other pieces of transportation equipment such as shipping containers or truck trailers on flatcars or special welled cars. These intermodal operations have led to a large increase in rail carriers' revenues, especially in the last decade.

Double-stack container trains are especially efficient because they can transport twice as much freight with the same amount of on-board labor and less fuel per ton-mile than a train with a single layer of containers.[23] These double-stack trains can run only on routes with high-clearance bridges overhead and limited mountainous topography. As a result, these operations are common in the United States but are rarer in China where the mountains impede their widespread adoption.[24]

Rail carriers in general have several competitive disadvantages compared to motor carriers. Rail networks are less dense than road networks partly because rail carriers are responsible for building their own tracks, while motor carriers can travel on (primarily) publicly funded roads. This results in fewer direct rail links between cities than roadways and necessitates more out-of-the-way switching operations. This in turn leads to longer and more unpredictable delivery times than customers can expect from motor carriers. In Europe, in particular, passenger traffic often takes precedence over international freight traffic on the rails, which further increases delivery times.[25] It is also possible that goods will have to stop at an international border to be switched to different equipment because the rail gauge between tracks in two adjacent countries can be different.[26] Studies have shown that many shippers value transit time and predictable service above all other factors in international transportation, so these long transit times put rail carriers at a distinct disadvantage.[27] Rail carriers are most competitive for long-distance moves where switching requirements are at a minimum, such as those from the West Coast of the United States to distribution hubs in the interior of the country.

Water

Water transportation encompasses moves on lakes and rivers, as well as on seas and oceans. Carriers often concentrate their service on one particular type of body of water, such as ocean carriers or river carriers, with specialized pieces of equipment designed for the particular body of water on which it will move. For example, ocean carriers often use gigantic container ships or tankers designed to carry a massive amount of freight over long distances on potentially rough ocean waters; on the other hand, carriers that operate on the Great Lakes in the United States have specially designed "laker" ships that are very long and narrow so they fit exactly into the locks between the lakes with only a few inches of clearance. River transportation is primarily conducted using unpowered barges that are connected and towed by tugboats. While ocean carriers haul freight of all kinds in their shipping containers, river barges primarily haul heavy bulk commodities such as iron, steel, coal, and grain due to their slow transit time and the fact that they are not enclosed to protect the goods from the weather. Thus river and lake carriers compete primarily with railroads; they are often cheaper than rail carriers but generally have longer transit times.[28]

It is impossible to overstate the importance of the development and adoption of the ocean container to the global economy. Before containerization, people had to load freight into ships' cargo holds largely by hand in individual pieces such as pallets or cartons. Some carriers provide this so-called break-bulk service today for shippers with individual units to ship, but it is limited because of the labor cost and the time it takes to handle the goods individually. Moving a loaded container, on the other hand, can be done very quickly with the use of a single crane at less than 10% of the cost of handling the goods inside the container individually. Ports can now unload and reload a ship carrying thousands of containers in less than a day, enabling the goods to continue their journey to the ultimate customer without being held up at the port for days.

These containers are standard size, which allows them to interact directly with other modes such as rail flatcars or road chassis. Without the standard design of the shipping container, intermodal transportation would require handling each piece of freight individually to transfer it from the ship to the railcar or trailer; this would eliminate all of the efficiencies that can be gained by having the modes work together. The shipping container is the backbone of international trade and allows us to live in a truly global economy.[29]

A major challenge affecting ocean transportation today is the shortage of capacity at ocean ports worldwide. The major bottleneck at ports is often not, in fact, the loading and unloading operation itself; instead, the bottleneck is the lack of intermodal rail and storage capacity at the port to facilitate movement of the containers out of the port area once they are unloaded from the vessel. Since these containers have nowhere to go, they fill the port area quickly and impede the unloading operation from moving as quickly as it can. As a result, many ports (and their local and state governments) are funding new intermodal tracks and terminals near the port to increase the capacity at this bottleneck.[30] Ocean carriers are also developing larger and larger container ships each year. Many of these megavessels are so large that the ocean floor at the port is not deep enough to accommodate them. Thus the government must dredge the ocean floor if it wants to handle these ships. Port dredging, though, has been criticized by many environmental groups because of its effect on the aquatic ecosystem at the coast. Thus port dredging has become a political battle throughout the world, with some areas supporting the projects and other areas rejecting them on environmental grounds. Carriers may need to adjust their routes so that these ships visit the deepest ports first and then unload at the shallower ports once they have deposited much of their total payload.[31]

While shippers have always had to plan for the risk of their goods being lost or damaged at sea during a long ocean voyage, another challenge has resurfaced recently that is perhaps more synonymous with the heyday of the British and Dutch East India companies: pirates. The major risk of ocean pirating today is centered around the Gulf of Aden, which is a vital throughway for those ships traveling from Asia to Europe and the United States through the Suez Canal. This is a critical route for petroleum and other bulk freight, as well as a growing container operation.

Pirates attacked over 100 ships in 2008, and as a result, major shipping companies are now charging a "war risk" fee up to US$100 per container for shipments that travel the route.[32] Shippers must consider this extra cost and the small possibility of their shipments being hijacked for an indefinite amount of time when they make their routing decisions.

Air

Air transportation is a primarily specialized form of transportation used to move small, high-value goods for which speed is of primary concern. Because air transportation is the most expensive mode in terms of cost per pound, the freight must justify this significant cost; otherwise, the goods can travel via truck or water. Often these items will either perish very quickly (such as cut flowers from Africa or South America) or are small and very expensive (such as diamonds or microprocessors). The latter would be too expensive to carry in inventory over a long transportation lead time that comes with other modes. Thus air carriers do not have much competition from other modes of transportation because of the unique service they provide.

Within the industry itself, however, competition is fierce between the carriers. This competition has only grown in recent years with the passage of many bilateral agreements known as *open skies agreements*, which allow the airlines from one country to provide service at the other country's airports.[33] The EU has allowed airlines from any member country to provide service at any airport within the EU since 1997.[34] Depending on the agreement, however, foreign airlines may not be able to engage in cabotage activities, where the airline starts and ends a route entirely within one country. International airline alliances with code-sharing agreements have evolved to give carriers the ability to sell an entire international itinerary on its own system yet still comply with the cabotage laws. This restriction on cabotage operations is also extended to ground and ocean transportation in many countries (including the United States).

Air carriers can also benefit from containerization in the same way that ocean carriers can. Containerization greatly reduces the handling required to load a piece of transportation equipment. Air carriers cannot, however, utilize the same containers used on ocean liners because their weight would take up too much of the plane's payload, leaving little capacity for the actual freight. Air freight containers are fashioned from lightweight material such as aluminum or even plywood to minimize the weight; as a result, these containers are used only to combine the freight into one package and not to provide protection. The shape and size of the containers are customized to fit into cargo holds on specific aircraft.[35]

A majority of air cargo travels on dedicated cargo planes, but a significant amount of freight also moves in the cargo holds of passenger airliners. Managing the cargo capacity on these passenger jets is among the most complicated tasks in transportation because the capacity available on each plane varies with the number of passengers and the amount of luggage. It is difficult for the carriers to predict how much capacity will be available for cargo on each flight, which affects the number of cargo bookings they can accept beforehand. Airlines have started to manage this capacity with revenue management techniques similar to those they use to price tickets for passengers. These techniques include the establishment of long-term contracts to guarantee certain levels of demand; customer segmentation to allocate capacity first to long-term, consistent shippers; and overbooking in case of excess available capacity or no-show freight.[36]

Pipeline

The final mode of transportation is pipeline transportation. Even though pipelines are often omitted from mainstream discussions of transportation, these carriers account for approximately 20% of the ton-miles of freight transported in the United States, which is a share comparable to that of water carriers.[37] This mode is an option only for several types of commodities such as oil, natural gas, and coal when it is mixed with water to form slurry. For applicable products, pipelines are the most efficient mode of transportation because they can move large amounts of freight with very few labor requirements. The freight is protected from theft because most of the pipelines are located underground, and the freight can also move continuously, 24 hours a day, instead of having to stop as a result of driver hours-of-service laws.[38]

International Transportation Intermediaries

The international transportation process can be very difficult for firms to navigate successfully. Scores of documentation requirements differ by the countries involved and even the specific freight or companies conducting the transaction. The freight often passes between several different transportation providers such as a foreign trucking company, an ocean carrier, a U.S. rail carrier, and a U.S. trucking company. The freight also interacts with customs and port officials located at two or more ports, each of which has its own rules and regulations that can be specific to the locale. There are so many special services that apply to international shipments that there are 13 different international commercial terms of sale—known as *Incoterms*—to specify which service charges are paid by the buyer and which are paid by the seller. Incoterms also designate which party is responsible for the risk of loss of the shipment at each stage in its journey.

Large organizations often staff a dedicated international transportation department in house that is responsible for completing required documentation, purchasing cargo insurance, and ensuring that shipments clear customs. A wide range of specialty service providers handles these tasks for smaller companies and larger ones that decide to outsource these functions to experts.[39] Some of these intermediaries also assist firms in a role similar to consultants to help them improve their transportation efficiency and consolidate shipments:

- *International freight forwarder.* International freight forwarders act as a general consultant on all matters and perform a wide range of specific functions for exporters, including shipment consolidation, preparing documentation, arranging for cargo insurance, advising on the acceptance of terms specified in letters of credit for export sales, and obtaining the consular documents that may be required to permit the goods to enter the foreign country as an import.
- *Non-vessel-operating common carrier (NVOCC).* NVOCCs are common carriers that purchase capacity on ocean vessels and consolidate small shipments into containers that use the purchased space. As a common carrier, an NVOCC takes title to

the freight that it accepts and is seen as the carrier in the eyes of the actual shippers; thus the NVOCC is also responsible for providing compensation for any losses or damages that occur in transit. Many NVOCCs also specialize in soliciting freight to prevent backhauls of empty containers that are needed at their origin point.

- *Customs broker.* Customs brokers ensure that goods pass through customs quickly at their point of import into a country by confirming compliance with local import laws and correct documentation and resolving any disputes that may arise. Customs brokers in the United States must pass a certification examination to perform their role.

- *Export management company (EMC).* The EMC performs many functions of international business for a firm including sales, marketing, financing, communication, and logistics. The EMC acts as the agent for the exporting firm and markets the exporter's products to a set of potential importing contacts abroad. Many EMCs specialize in selling to customers in one particular country and even one particular industry within that country to utilize its network most effectively. EMCs often work closely with international freight forwarders (or are even extensions of the freight forwarders' operations) to ensure effective importing of the product into the foreign country.

- *Export trading company (ETC).* The ETC purchases products from exporting firms and resells these items in foreign countries. These companies are different from EMCs, which are only agents for the exporter and receive a commission, because they actually own the products that they sell in the foreign country. ETCs are a good way for new exporters to enter the international marketplace, but firms should establish their own exporting operations if they want to commit to the strategy long term.

- *Export packer.* Export packers are specialists that design product packaging to protect the freight during its often long and difficult international journey. These firms can also build specialized packaging with removable flaps and slots to allow customs officials to inspect the freight without opening and destroying the packaging. Since many transportation rates and some customs duties are assessed based on the weight of the item including the packaging, the export packer can ensure that the packaging is as light and small as it can be while still providing the necessary amount of protection for the freight.

Global Warehousing and Distribution Management

Many of the major issues related to structuring international distribution operations can be grouped into two major categories: network design and warehouse operations. The first category considers high-level strategic decisions such as facility location and methods of distribution to the final customers. The second category looks at issues specifically related to operations within a facility itself.

Network design decisions in a global supply chain are very similar to those domestically, except that there are even more issues to consider. Firms desiring to serve a foreign market will usually establish a distribution presence, if not a manufacturing presence as well, in the region so that customers can be served within a few days from stocks of inventory kept in local distribution centers instead of relying on international shipments to fulfill each foreign order. The company often has many options with respect to the number and actual location of the distribution facilities in the foreign market. Common criteria for the global distribution network design decision include[40]

- tariffs and duties;
- nontariff trade barriers;
- exchange rate;
- corporate income tax in the foreign country;
- transportation time and cost for supply shipments and for distribution to customers;
- convenient access to transportation rights-of-way such as highway junctions, airports and seaports, railroad switching terminals, and rivers or lakes;
- inventory cost for goods stored in the distribution centers;
- availability and cost of skilled workers for the facility.

Firms should continue to adopt a supply chain orientation with respect to their logistics and distribution decisions, thereby considering more comprehensive supply chain costs instead of conducting a myopic analysis based solely on optimizing one portion of the supply chain. These global supply chain design processes should include planning for multiple echelons of production and distribution at the same time.[41] This would ensure that the firm's logistics network was well positioned with respect to its suppliers, production facilities and subcontractors, distribution centers, and major customers.

The network design process should also include consideration and placement of reverse logistics operations.[42] All organizations receive items returned by their customers for many different reasons. In some parts of the world, especially Europe, manufacturers are required by law to take their products back from their customers at the end of the product's useful life and dispose of the product in an environmentally responsible way. Methods of disposal include repair, remanufacturing, and materials reclamation in addition to sending unusable materials to a landfill. This is the case in the electronics industry in Europe as a result of the Waste Electrical and Electronic Equipment (WEEE) legislation adopted by the EU in 2002 and 2003. Regardless of how firms process their returned items and the reason for the returns, the firms must develop a strategy to cope with them in the most efficient way. Some firms have even been able to turn their reverse logistics operations into a profitable part of their business through remanufacturing or using returned items as an inexpensive source of materials in the production of new items. Companies should integrate the location of these reverse logistics and related processes into the design of their overall supply chain network to devise the best overall structure for the entire system.

Another factor that has forever changed distribution is the widespread adoption of the Internet.[43] No longer is a customer restricted to the product selection available in his or her local stores. Now customers can order a wide range of products from centralized sellers that are able to stock much more variety than they could afford to stock in a single store. The Internet aggregates geographically dispersed demand for products that would not make a bestseller list, justifying the centralized supplier's stocking decision. Selling one or two of an item each month is not profitable if the cost of storing the item is high. Digital distribution of media such as music, e-books, and movies has further decreased inventory and distribution costs, making it possible for firms to reach the "long tail" of demand and increasing the consumers' ability to purchase products that better fit their particular preferences and interests.

Managing warehousing operations around the world is often similar to managing production in global sites.[44] Automation is usually low in countries such as India and China where the labor cost is relatively low. Warehousing in Western Europe or the United States, on the other hand, is often highly automated because of the high cost of labor. In Germany and France, in particular, there is even more incentive for companies to automate their warehousing operations because the labor force is highly inflexible due to rules on vacation, length of the workday, and the inability of companies to lay off workers easily if they want or need to reduce capacity. Many warehouses have only one level, but in countries such as Singapore and Japan where land is scarce and expensive, multilevel warehouses are more common.

Transportation Infrastructure

The condition of the transportation infrastructure in various locations around the world has a great impact on the supply chain operations of the companies doing business in the area. Poor infrastructure adds variability to the supply chain, making the supply chain harder to manage. Firms shipping products from the Cloud Forest in Ecuador occasionally experience a delay of a day or two on their shipments reaching the port of Guayaquil when the only road out of the Andes Mountains is blocked by a rockslide. There is no alternate route, so the freight must sit and wait (and possibly miss its loading time on a ship). Companies must develop ways to deal with longer travel times and breakdowns of equipment. Often they absorb these shocks by carrying extra inventory, but these infrastructure problems could be significant enough to drive firms away from the country altogether. Warehouses in countries with poor transportation infrastructure must be located closer to their customers to reduce the lead time for shipments of customers' orders. This would require the firm to establish more, smaller warehouses than perhaps it can support profitably and could drive the firm to another location that is more suitable.[45] Recall that transit time and predictable delivery are among the most important factors for firms selecting a transportation provider; it should be no surprise that these are also important considerations for those deciding *where* to locate a foreign operation.[46]

Transportation infrastructure spending is an important political issue around the world. The infrastructure for most modes of transportation such as road, air, and water is built and maintained by the government. Only rail and pipeline carriers are responsible for establishing their own rights-of-way, which greatly increases their fixed costs and provides a barrier to entry to the market. The other carriers pay for the use of the publicly funded infrastructure through taxes, tolls, landing fees, and dock fees that reflect their level of volume.

A developed transportation structure is inseparable from a country's economic prosperity. Research has shown a strong correlation between a country's transportation infrastructure and its long-term economic growth.[47] Mexico, for instance, lags far behind its North American counterparts in infrastructure spending, yet its logistics networks are largely superior to those of the Caribbean countries; this is exactly its economy's position as well. In light of the previous findings, it is discouraging to see that Mexico's total spending on transportation infrastructure was lower in 2003 than it was in 1995.[48]

Many countries have, in contrast, largely increased their spending on transportation infrastructure in an attempt to grow their economy. India, which has long suffered from substandard infrastructure and still suffers in many regions today, has committed to investing over US$450 billion from 2007 to 2012 to upgrade its transportation capabilities.[49] China has recently spent more than US$120 billion per year on improving its road network alone, with the goal of eclipsing the total highway miles that cover the United States.[50] Firms should monitor the current infrastructure and planned investments around the world to identify new opportunities for market expansion with improved infrastructure or potential risks that would necessitate a shift to a new supplier located elsewhere in the world.

Example 4.3. Kola Real's International Expansion Strategy

In the 1980s the city of Ayacucho, Peru, was under the control of a terrorist group called the "Shining Path." These guerrilla forces would not allow trucks carrying foreign goods to enter the region and would regularly hijack any trucks attempting to make such a delivery. The founders of the Ajegroup Corporation spotted a market opportunity due to the scarcity of soft drinks such as Coca-Cola and Pepsi caused by this terrorist embargo; in 1988 they started selling a soft drink called Kola Real in old beer bottles, using start-up funds obtained from a second mortgage on their house.

After the guerrilla activity died down in the 1990s, Kola Real continued to flourish. The product had found its place as a low-cost competitor in the market. Peru had many soft drinks available, but most of the imported products targeted a higher class customer who could afford relatively expensive luxury items. Kola Real, on the other hand, continued to appeal to the majority of Peruvians who were poor by keeping their costs and prices low. The company was able to keep costs at a minimum by manufacturing its own products (unlike Coca-Cola and Pepsi bottlers, which had to pay up to 20% of their revenues to purchase concentrates from the parent companies). The Ajegroup Corporation also outsourced its delivery services rather than maintaining its own fleet of trucks that would have to navigate difficult terrain. Some of the third-party transportation providers were simply individuals with old pickup trucks or whatever was available but could perform the delivery adequately. The firm eschewed the trend in the cola wars to overspend on advertising, instead relying primarily on word-of-mouth advertising to promote its product.

Distributing the soft drinks in plastic as opposed to glass bottles was another innovation that helped Kola Real compete with the international brands and fueled its own global expansion efforts. Plastic bottles are much less expensive to produce than glass bottles, and they can be made in a larger size to be sold in supermarkets. The international brands such as Coca-Cola and Pepsi primarily sold single-serve bottles in small, local stores at the time. The plastic bottles allowed

Kola Real to find a home in the new supermarkets established throughout Latin America.

This low-cost strategy helped Kola Real succeed in its expansion outside of Peru to Venezuela, Ecuador, Mexico, and Costa Rica. By 2004 the annual sales worldwide were US$50 million, and foreign sales outside of Peru (especially in Mexico) accounted for approximately 70% of the total sales. The success of Kola Real shows how firms that know their market well can succeed even when facing infrastructure challenges, and it provides a reminder that companies can also be profitable by serving the needs of poorer consumers.

Source: Robertson (2008).

Chapter Summary

This chapter has discussed the major strategies for organizing international distribution operations, the modes of international transportation and the specialists that help firms with the import and export processes, considerations for designing and operating a global distribution network, and the importance of transportation infrastructure in global logistics. Key takeaways from this chapter include the following:

- Firms looking to establish global distribution operations have several major decisions to make. They must consider whether or not they will customize their products to suit the tastes of a foreign market, how much risk of investment loss they are willing to tolerate, and how much control over their foreign operations they want to maintain from the home office.
- Transit time and reliability are among the most important factors that international shippers consider when they select a transportation mode and a specific carrier.
- Companies should design their global supply chain networks holistically by simultaneously considering potential supplier locations, manufacturing plant locations, warehouse and distribution center locations, and major customer locations. This will ensure that the entire system is optimized and will

not require a redesign for at least 5 or 10 years because it is often expensive to accommodate large shifts in distribution networks.

• Firms should consider the state of the transportation infrastructure in the countries over which their global supply chain network spans because poor infrastructure can introduce variability into transit times and often requires firms to carry extra inventory as a result.

Notes

Chapter 1

1. Issenberg (2007), p. 40.

2. Even firms engaged in local sourcing could purchase office supplies or cleaning products that were manufactured abroad, so technically they have a global supply chain in this respect. We usually consider only the source of the major product components when we consider their origin, however, not these administrative or maintenance items.

3. As quoted in Mentzer, Stank, and Esper (2008), p. 32.

4. Supply Chain Council, http://www.supply-chain.org

5. Moving on up (2009).

6. This timeline perspective of the development of supply chain management is based on Coyle, Langley, Gibson, Novack, and Bardi (2009).

7. Unfortunately, much research has shown that functional silos still exist to some extent in many organizations today. See, for example, Shub and Stonebraker (2009) and Ross (2006).

8. Fine (1998).

9. The discussion of the bullwhip effect is based on Lee, Padmanabhan, and Whang (1997a) and Lee, Padmanabhan, and Whang (1997b). Technically, the bullwhip effect was identified by Jay Forrester (1961) and his colleagues in the field of industrial dynamics in the early 1960s, but P&G's study popularized the notion and precipitated much of the recent interest in the field of supply chain management.

10. Cachon and Lariviere (1999).

11. Lee (2004).

12. Incentive alignment mechanisms for supply chains have drawn considerable interest from academic researchers and practitioners. Tsay, Nahmias, and Agrawal (1999) provide an excellent review of the basic methods of coordinating the supply chain by realigning incentives.

13. Van Hoek and Mitchell (2006).

14. Maiga, Jacobs, and Koufteros (2010).

15. Van Hoek and Mitchell (2006).

16. To illustrate this point, Fine (1998) provides many examples of industries where the market leader has changed hands many times over the course of a few decades. Regardless of whether the industry has a fast rate of change (such as the

electronics industry) or a slow rate of change (such as the commercial aviation industry), no company can expect to dominate a given industry in the long run.

17. Cargille and Fry (2006).

18. Slone (2004).

19. Nonino and Panizzolo (2007).

20. Norek, Gass, and Jorgenson (2007).

21. Quesada, Rachamadugu, Gonzalez, and Martinez (2008).

22. Monahan and Nardone (2007).

Chapter 2

1. These types of restaurants are currently increasing in popularity all over the world, sometimes more out of necessity because of a lack of transportation infrastructure (such as in India) and often because of an increased social consciousness of the negative environmental impact of transportation and health concerns over genetically modified meat and produce.

2. Yung, Lee, and Lai (2009).

3. Note that service companies as well as the restaurant in our example cannot use the strategy of carrying extra inventory to buffer large amounts of variation. Services cannot usually be produced ahead of their desired consumption time, and restaurants suffer from perishability issues with fresh ingredients over long periods of time.

4. Mercier, Sirkin, and Bratton (2010).

5. See Rivoli (2009) for complete details about the supply chain for T-shirts.

6. Ogg and Kanellos (2007); Vizio (2011).

7. Ferreira and Prokopets (2009).

8. McCarter and Northcraft (2007).

9. The discussion of the casino industry is based on Taleb (2010).

10. Hauser (2003).

11. Sheffi and Rice (2005).

12. Handfield, Blackhurst, and Elkins (2008).

13. Morehouse and Cardoso (2011).

14. These suggestions for assessing a supply chain's vulnerability are based on Hauser (2003) and Sheffi and Rice (2005).

15. Indeed, a major U.S. manufacturer engaged researchers in my department a few years ago to help them map their supply chain. It was surprising that such a large company did not have a complete picture of its tiers of supply and the customers in its extended distribution channel.

16. While there are specialized software packages that perform Monte Carlo simulations, spreadsheet add-ins such as Oracle's Crystal Ball or Palisade's @Risk provide a great deal of analytical power for risk analysis at a reasonable cost for even small businesses without requiring that the analyst have knowledge of a specialized software program.

17. This discussion of supply chain resilience is based on Sheffi and Rice (2005); Tang (2006); and Christopher, Mena, Khan, and Yurt (2011).

18. The Boston Consulting Group study is found in Mercier, Sirkin, and Bratton (2010). Some additional ways to increase agility are found in Sheffi and Rice (2005) and Tang (2006).

19. Sheffi and Rice (2005); Christopher et al. (2011).

20. Sheffi and Rice (2005); Tang (2006); Mercier et al. (2010); Christopher et al. (2011).

21. Hauser (2003).

22. Henrich, Khanna, and Ozkaya (2011).

23. The discussion of the three security initiatives is largely based on Barone (2008).

24. The CBP has also recently instituted a similar program, known as Global Entry, for frequent air travelers to bypass the usually long lines at U.S. passport control and enter the United States more quickly.

25. Saphir (2007).

26. Management Dynamics (2011).

27. Management Dynamics (2011).

28. This discussion of traceability in the supply chain is based on Siegfried (2011).

Chapter 3

1. This discussion of the strategic importance of the make versus buy decision within procurement is based on Fine (1998).

2. If you want to check your ability to recall your calculus training, the correct answer is 21.

3. Recall that IBM did introduce its own OS/2 operating system to compete with Microsoft Windows, but the product gained little traction as Windows became the de facto system in the market.

4. Gilley and Rasheed (2000).

5. Lindholm and Suomala (2007); Young, Swan, Thomchick, and Ruamsook (2009).

6. Platts and Song (2010).

7. Young et al. (2009).

8. This discussion of total unit cost is based on Harding (2007).

9. Ferreira and Prokopets (2009).

10. This discussion of shifting Chinese manufacturing operations inland to the west is based on Dieter (2010). The *Hukou* system refers to the household registration system in China that identifies a person as a resident of a region and requires that rural citizens have a permit if they want to migrate to a city.

11. Ferreira and Prokopets (2009).

12. Murphy (2008).

13. Wahyuni, Ghauri, and Karsten (2007).

14. Minkov and Hofstede (2011).

15. The first two recommendations in this list are based on Wahyuni et al. (2007). The remaining strategies are based on Trent and Monczka (2005).

16. These final three recommendations also apply to establishing alliances with a domestic supply chain partner.

17. Wahyuni et al. (2007).

18. Grossler (2010).

19. See, for example, Karnes and Karnes (2000); Su, Chang, and Ferguson (2005); and Miemczyk and Howard (2008).

20. Pretious and Love (2006).

21. Pretious and Love (2006); Harney (2008).

22. Ellis (2008).

23. Presutti and Mawhinney (2009).

24. De Boer, Labro, and Morlacchi (2001).

25. Bhutta and Huq (2002); Cebi and Bayraktar (2003); Liu and Hai (2005).

26. Ting and Cho (2008).

27. Lin and Juang (2008).

28. These and more examples of bias in procurement decisions can be found in Carter, Kaufmann, and Michel (2007).

29. Kaufmann, Carter, and Buhrmann (2010).

30. Day, Magnan, Webb, and Hughes (2008).

31. Trent and Monczka (2005); Wahyuni et al. (2007); Mascarenhas and Koza (2008).

32. This section about network orchestrators is based on Magretta (1998) and Fung, Fung, and Wind (2008).

33. Weitzman (2011).

34. Drake and Schlachter (2008).

35. Watts and Hahn (1993).

36. Wagner (2006).

37. Liker and Choi (2004); Drake and Schlachter (2008).

38. Ghijsen, Semeijn, and Ernstson (2010).

39. Simatupang and Sridharan (2002).

40. This discussion of quick response is based on Drake and Marley (2010).

41. This discussion of vendor-managed inventory (VMI) programs is based on Sari (2007).

42. Raskin (2003); Kurtulus and Toktay (2005).

43. Raskin (2003).

44. Morgan, Kaleka, and Gooner (2008).

45. Kurtulus and Toktay (2005).

46. Steermann (2003).

Chapter 4

1. To understand how frustrating this difference can be, try typing on a keyboard in Germany that has switched the position of the "Z" and "Y" keys.

2. This section is based largely on Gourdin (2006) and David and Stewart (2008).

3. Individuals can reach global customers through websites such as eBay and other consumer-to-consumer online marketplaces.

4. David and Stewart (2008) note, however, that people do not necessarily need a licensing agreement to produce a counterfeit product. For example, most U.S. patents are openly available online. As a result, the risk of piracy may be a greater concern for *any* owner of intellectual property and not a risk specific to licensors.

5. Lakshman (2009).

6. Mangan, Lalwani, and Butcher (2008).

7. Coyle, Novack, Gibson, and Bardi (2011).

8. McKinnon (2006).

9. Of course, the facility location decision process should consider factors such as the proximity to transportation rights-of-way. It is no coincidence that many airports have large industrial parks located nearby. Similarly, most if not all of the steel mills located in Pittsburgh during its steel-producing heyday were located on the banks of the city's three rivers.

10. Gourdin (2006).

11. LaFranchi (2011).

12. Albright and Lo (2009).

13. Wu and Dunn (1995).

14. Proctor (2006).

15. Loudin and Mazel (2011a).

16. Wilson (2011).

17. Browne, Allen, and Woodburn (2007).

18. Examples of these models include Custodio and Oliveira (2006); Moura and Oliveira (2009); and Merrick and Bookbinder (2010).

19. The first four recommendations in this list are based on Cubitt (2002).

20. This recommendation is based on Mollenkopf and Tate (2011).

21. This recommendation is based on Disney, Potter, and Gardner (2003).

22. This recommendation is based on McKinnon (2007).

23. Gourdin (2006).

24. Wang (2007).

25. Lewis, Semeijn, and Vellenga (2001).

26. Gourdin (2006).

27. Vanek and Smith (2004); Shawdon (2006).

28. Gourdin (2006).

29. Levinson (2006).

30. Quinn (2007).

31. Loudin and Mazel (2011b).

32. Boyanton and Geary (2009).

33. David and Stewart (2008).

34. Gourdin (2006).

35. David and Stewart (2008).

36. Becker and Dill (2007).

37. Coyle et al. (2011).

38. Gourdin (2006).

39. This discussion of international intermediaries is based on Gourdin (2006); Mangan et al. (2008); David and Stewart (2008); and Coyle et al. (2011).

40. These criteria for the global supply chain network design decision are based on Meixell and Gargeya (2005); Mentzer (2008); and Melo, Nickel, and Saldanha-da-Gama (2009).

41. Meixell and Gargeya (2005).

42. This discussion of reverse logistics is based on Drake and Ferguson (2008).

43. This discussion of the Internet and its effect on reaching the "long tail" of customers is based on Anderson (2006).

44. This discussion of the difference in warehousing operations around the world is based on Bartholdi and Hackman (2011).

45. Bartholdi and Hackman (2011).

46. Vanek and Smith (2004); Shawdon (2006).

47. Calderon and Serven (2004).

48. Myers, Fawcett, and Smith (2002); Drake and Rojo (2008).

49. Kilgore, Joseph, and Metersky (2007); Leahy (2008).

50. Gourdin (2006).

References

Albright, D., & Lo, A. (2009). Transportation management's role in supply chain excellence. *Supply Chain Management Review 13*(7), S52–S62.

Anderson, C. (2006). *The long tail.* New York, NY: Hyperion.

Atwater, C., Gopalan, R., Lancioni, R., & Hunt, J. (2010). To change or not to change: How motor carriers responded following 9/11. *Journal of Business Logistics 31*(2), 129–155.

Baida, Z., Rukanova, B., Tan, Y.-H., & Wigand, R. T. (2007). Heineken shows benefits of customs collaboration. *Supply Chain Management Review 11*(7), 11–12.

Barone, A. (2008). Protecting the homeland: Homeland security issues for importation to the United States. *CSCMP Explores . . . 5*(Summer), 1–11.

Bartholdi, J. J., III, & Hackman, S. T. (2011). *Warehouse & distribution science* (Release 0.94). Retrieved July 28, 2011, from Warehouse-Science: http://www.warehouse-science.com

Becker, B., & Dill, N. (2007). Managing the complexity of air cargo revenue management. *Journal of Revenue and Pricing Management 6*(3), 175–187.

Bhutta, K. S., & Huq, F. (2002). Supplier selection problem: A comparison of total cost of ownership and Analytic Hierarchy Process approaches. *Supply Chain Management: An International Journal 7*(3), 126–135.

Boyanton, E., & Geary, S. (2009). Danger on the high seas. *Supply Chain Quarterly 3*(4). Retrieved July 28, 2011, from CSCMP's Supply Chain Quarterly: http://www.supplychainquarterly.com/topics/Logistics/scq200904piracy

Browne, M., Allen, J., & Woodburn, A. (2007). Developments in Western European logistics strategies. In D. Waters (Ed.), *Global logistics* (5th ed., pp. 353–373). London, UK: Kogan Page.

Cachon, G. P., & Lariviere, M. A. (1999). Capacity allocation using past sales: When to turn-and-earn. *Management Science 45*(5), 685–703.

Cadilhon, J.-J., & Fearne, A. P. (2005). Lessons in collaboration: A case study from Vietnam. *Supply Chain Management Review 9*(4), 11–12.

Calderon, C., & Serven, L. (2004). *The effects of infrastructure development on growth and income distribution* (World Bank Policy Research Working Paper No. 3400). Washington, DC: The World Bank.

Cargille, B., & Fry, C. (2006). Design for supply chain: Spreading the word across HP. *Supply Chain Management Review 10*(5), 34–41.

Carter, C. R., Kaufmann, L., & Michel, A. (2007). Behavioral supply management: A taxonomy of judgment and decision-making biases. *International Journal of Physical Distribution & Logistics Management 37*(8), 631–669.

Cebi, F., & Bayraktar, D. (2003). An integrated approach for supplier selection. *Logistics Information Management 16*, 395–400.

Christopher, M., Mena, C., Khan, O., & Yurt, O. (2011). Approaches to managing global sourcing risk. *Supply Chain Management: An International Journal 16*(2), 67–81.

Cooke, J. A. (2008). Control is instrumental to Teradyne's success. *Supply Chain Quarterly 2*(3). Retrieved July 31, 2011, from CSCMP's Supply Chain Quarterly: http://www.supplychainquarterly.com/print/scq200803teradyne

Cooke, J. A. (2007). Running inventory like a Deere. *Supply Chain Quarterly 1*(3), 46–50.

Cooke, J. A. (2011). Sharing supply chains for mutual gain. *Supply Chain Quarterly 5*(2). Retrieved July 31, 2011, from CSCMP's Supply Chain Quarterly: http://www.supplychainquarterly.com/topics/Global/scq201102kimberly

Coyle, J. J., Langley, C. J., Jr., Gibson, B. L., Novack, R. A., & Bardi, E. J. (2009). *Supply chain management: A logistics perspective* (8th ed.). Mason, OH: South-Western Cengage Learning.

Coyle, J. J., Novack, R. A., Gibson, B. J., & Bardi, E. J. (2011). *Transportation: A supply chain perspective* (7th ed.). Mason, OH: South-Western Cengage Learning.

Cubitt, B. (2002). Cutting the fat on freight. *APICS—The Performance Advantage* (March), 43–45.

Custodio, A. L., & Oliveira, R. C. (2006). Redesigning distribution operations: A case study on integrating inventory management and vehicle routes design. *International Journal of Logistics: Research and Applications 9*(2), 169–187.

David, P. A., & Stewart, R. D. (2008). *International logistics* (2nd ed.). Mason, OH: Thomson-Atomic Dog.

Day, M., Magnan, G., Webb, M., & Hughes, J. (2008). Strategic supplier relationship management. *Supply Chain Management Review 12*(4), 40–48.

De Boer, L., Labro, E., & Morlacchi, P. (2001). A review of methods supporting supplier selection. *European Journal of Purchasing and Supply Management 7*, 75–89.

de Kok, T., Janssen, F., van Doremalen, J., van Wachem, E., Clerkx, M., & Peeters, W. (2005). Philips Electronics synchronizes its supply chain to end the bullwhip effect. *Interfaces 35*(1), 37–48.

Dieter, P. (2010). "Go west" into China . . . carefully. *Supply Chain Quarterly 4*(3). Retrieved July 28, 2011, from CSCMP's Supply Chain Quarterly: http://www.supplychainquarterly.com/topics/Logistics/scq2010china

Disney, S. M., Potter, A. T., & Gardner, B. M. (2003). The impact of vendor managed inventory on transport operations. *Transportation Research Part E 39*, 363–380.

Drake, M. J., & Ferguson, M. E. (2008). Closed-loop supply chain management for global sustainability. In J. A. F. Stoner & C. Wankel (Eds.), *Global sustainability initiatives: New models and new approaches* (pp. 173–191). Charlotte, NC: Information Age Publishers.

Drake, M. J., & Marley, K. A. (2010). The evolution of Quick Response programs. In T. C. E. Cheng & T.-S. Choi (Eds.), *Innovative quick response programs in logistics & supply chain management* (pp. 3–22). Heidelberg, Germany: Springer.

Drake, M. J., & Rojo, N. D. (2008). The current state of Mexican logistics operations. *Journal of International Management Studies 3*(2), 92–97.

Drake, M. J., & Schlachter, J. T. (2008). A virtue-ethics analysis of supply chain collaboration. *Journal of Business Ethics 82*(4), 851–864.

Ellis, S. (2008). The case for "profitable proximity." *Supply Chain Quarterly 2*(3), 56–62.

Ferreira, J., & Prokopets, L. (2009). Does offshoring still make sense? *Supply Chain Management Review 13*(1), 20–27.

Fine, C. H. (1998). *Clockspeed: Winning industry control in the age of temporary advantage.* New York, NY: Basic Books.

Forrester, J. (1961). *Industrial dynamics.* New York, NY: MIT Press and John Wiley & Sons.

Fung, V., Fung, W., & Wind, J. (2008). *Competing in a flat world: Building enterprises for a borderless world.* Upper Saddle River, NJ: Prentice Hall.

Ghijsen, P. W. T., Semeijn, J., & Ernstson, S. (2010). Supplier satisfaction and commitment: The role of influence strategies and supplier development. *Journal of Purchasing & Supply Management 16*, 17–26.

Gilley, K. M., & Rasheed, A. (2000). Making more by doing less: An analysis of outsourcing and its effects on firm performance. *Journal of Management 26*(4), 763–790.

Gourdin, K. N. (2006). *Global logistics management* (2nd ed.). Malden, MA: Blackwell.

Grossler, A. (2010). The development of strategic manufacturing capabilities in emerging and developed markets. *Operations Management Research 3*, 60–67.

Handfield, R. B., Blackhurst, J., & Elkins, D. (2008). A framework for reducing the impact of disruptions to the supply chain: Observations from multiple executives. In R. B. Handfield & K. McCormack (Eds.), *Supply chain risk management* (pp. 29–49). Boca Raton, FL: Auerbach.

Harding, M. L. (2007). Gauging total cost, supplier by supplier. *Supply Chain Quarterly 1*(3), 64–68.

Harney, A. (2008). *The China price: The true cost of Chinese competitive advantage*. New York, NY: Penguin Press.

Hauser, L. M. (2003). Risk-adjusted supply chain management. *Supply Chain Management Review 7*(6), 64–71.

Henrich, J., Khanna, N., & Ozkaya, E. (2011). Improve your odds. *Supply Chain Quarterly 5*(1), 40–46.

Issenberg, I. (2007). *The sushi economy*. New York, NY: Gotham Books.

Karnes, C. L., & Karnes, L. R. (2000). Ross Controls: A case study in mass customization. *Production and Inventory Management Journal 41*(3), 1–4.

Kaufmann, L., Carter, C. R., & Buhrmann, C. (2010). Debiasing the supplier selection decision: A taxonomy and conceptualization. *International Journal of Physical Distribution & Logistics Management 40*(10), 792–821.

Kilgore, M., Joseph, A., & Metersky, J. (2007). The logistical challenges of doing business in India. *Supply Chain Management Review 11*(7), 36–43.

Kilzer, L. (2011, April 3). Apple tries to avoid Motorola's mistakes in China. Retrieved July 31, 2011, from *Pittsburgh Tribune Review*: http://www.pittsburghlive.com/x/pittsburghtrib/news/nation-world/s_730463.html

Kurtulus, M., & Toktay, L. B. (2005). Category captainship: Who wins, who loses? *ECR Journal 5*(1), 59–65.

LaFranchi, H. (2011, July 6). Landmark US-Mexico trucking agreement resolves 15-year conflict. Retrieved July 26, 2011, from *Christian Science Monitor*: http://www.csmonitor.com/USA/Foreign-Policy/2011/0706/Landmark-US-Mexico-trucking-agreement-resolves-15-year-conflict

Lakshman, N. (2009). Why Wal-Mart's first India store isn't a Wal-Mart. Retrieved July 26, 2011, from *Time*: http://www.time.com/time/world/article/0,8599,1898823,00.html

Leahy, J. (2008, June 30). A passage through India. *Financial Times* (U.S. edition), 7.

Lee, H. L. (2004). The triple-A supply chain. *Harvard Business Review 82*(10), 103–112.

Lee, H. L., Padmanabhan, V., & Whang, S. (1997a). The bullwhip effect in supply chains. *MIT Sloan Management Review 38*(3), 93–102.

Lee, H. L., Padmanabhan, V., & Whang, S. (1997b). Information distortion in a supply chain: The bullwhip effect. *Management Science 43*(4), 546–558.

Levinson, M. (2006). *The box: How the shipping container made the world smaller and the world economy bigger*. Princeton, NJ: Princeton University Press.

Lewis, I., Semeijn, J., & Vellenga, D. B. (2001). Issues and initiatives surrounding rail freight transportation in Europe. *Transportation Journal 41*(2/3), 23–31.

Liker, J. K., & Choi, T. Y. (2004). Building deep supplier relationships. *Harvard Business Review 82*(12), 104–113.

Lin, S.-S., & Juang, Y.-S. (2008). Selecting green suppliers with Analytic Hierarchy Process for biotechnology industry. *Operations and Supply Chain Management 1*(2), 115–129.

Lindholm, A., & Suomala, P. (2007). Learning by costing: Sharpening cost image through life cycle costing? *International Journal of Productivity and Performance Measurement 56*(8), 651–672.

Liu, F. H., & Hai, H. L. (2005). The Voting Analytic Hierarchy Process method for selecting suppliers. *International Journal of Production Economics 97*, 308–317.

Loudin, A., & Mazel, J. (2011a). Drivers hours of service law. *WERCSheet 34*(2), 4–5.

Loudin, A., & Mazel, J. (2011b). The new big dig. *WERCSheet 34*(2), 1–3, 5.

Magretta, J. (1998). Fast, global, and entrepreneurial: Supply chain management, Hong Kong style. *Harvard Business Review 76*(5), 102–114.

Maiga, A. S., Jacobs, F. A., & Koufteros, X. A. (2010). Supply chain integration: The effects on competitive capability and financial performance. *Proceedings of the 2010 Supply Chain Management Educators' Conference.* Retrieved July 7, 2011, from the Council of Supply Chain Management Professionals: http://cscmp.org/downloads/public/academics/10scmec/presentation3.pdf

Management Dynamics. (2011). 10+2 vital facts about the importer security filing. Retrieved July 28, 2011, from Management Dynamics: http://www.managementdynamics.com/html/rl_white_papers.html

Mangan, J., Lalwani, C., & Butcher, T. (2008). *Global logistics and supply chain management.* West Sussex, UK: John Wiley & Sons.

Mascarenhas, B., & Koza, M. P. (2008). Develop and nurture an international alliance capability. *Thunderbird International Business Review 50*(2), 121–128.

McCarter, M. W., & Northcraft, G. B. (2007). Happy together? Insights and implications of viewing managed supply chains as a social dilemma. *Journal of Operations Management 25*, 498–511.

McKinnon, A. C. (2006). Life without trucks: The impact of a temporary disruption of road freight transport on a national economy. *Journal of Business Logistics 27*(2), 227–250.

McKinnon, A. C. (2007). Road transport optimization. In D. Waters (Ed.), *Global logistics* (5th ed., pp. 273–289). London, UK: Kogan Page.

Meixell, M. J., & Gargeya, V. B. (2005). Global supply chain design: A literature review and critique. *Transportation Research Part E 41*, 531–550.

Melo, M. T., Nickel, S., & Saldanha-da-Gama, F. (2009). Facility location and supply chain management—A review. *European Journal of Operational Research 196*, 401–412.

Mentzer, J. T. (2008). 7 keys to facility location. *Supply Chain Management Review 12*(5), 25–31.

Mentzer, J. T., Stank, T. P., & Esper, T. L. (2008). Supply chain management and its relationship to logistics, marketing, production, and operations management. *Journal of Business Logistics 29*(1), 31–46.

Mercier, P., Sirkin, H., & Bratton, J. (2010). 8 ways to boost supply chain agility. *Supply Chain Management Review 14*(1), 18–25.

Merrick, R. J., & Bookbinder, J. H. (2010). Environmental assessment of shipment release policies. *International Journal of Physical Distribution & Logistics Management 40*(10), 748–762.

Miemczyk, J., & Howard, M. (2008). Supply strategies for build-to-order: Managing global auto operations. *Supply Chain Management: An International Journal 13*(1), 3–8.

Minkov, M., & Hofstede, G. (2011). The evolution of Hofstede's doctrine. *Cross-Cultural Management: An International Journal 18*(1), 10–20.

Mollenkopf, D. A., & Tate, W. L. (2011). Green and lean supply chains. *CSCMP Explores . . . 8*(Spring), 1–18.

Monahan, S., & Nardone, R. (2007). How Unilever aligned its supply chain and business strategies. *Supply Chain Management Review 11*(8), 44–50.

Morehouse, J. E., & Cardoso, L. (2011). Consumer product fraud—How to stop it now. *Supply Chain Quarterly 5*(2), 24–31.

Morgan, N. A., Kaleka, A., & Gooner, R. A. (2008). Focal supplier opportunism in supermarket retailer category management. *Journal of Operations Management 25*, 512–527.

Moura, A., & Oliveira, J. F. (2009). An integrated approach to the vehicle routing and container loading problems. *OR Spectrum 31*(4), 775–800.

Moving on up: Is the recession heralding a return to Henry Ford's model? (2009, March 27). *The Economist.* Retrieved July 28, 2011, from http://www.economist.com/node/13173671

Murphy, S. (2008). Will sourcing come closer to home? *Supply Chain Management Review 12*(6), 33–37.

Myers, M. B., Fawcett, S. E., & Smith, S. R. (2002). International production sharing opportunities in Mexico and the Caribbean: A comparative study of manufacturing and logistics efforts. *Latin American Business Review 3*(2), 65–84.

Nonino, F., & Panizzolo, R. (2007). Integrated production/distribution planning in the supply chain: The Febal case study. *Supply Chain Management: An International Journal 12*(2), 150–163.

Norek, C. D., Gass, W., & Jorgenson, T. (2007). SMB? You can transform your supply chain, too. *Supply Chain Management Review 11*(2), 32–38.

Ogg, E., & Kanellos, M. (2007). *The secret of Vizio's success.* Retrieved June 16, 2011, from CNet News: http://news.cnet.com/The-secret-of-Vizios -success/2100–1041_3–6203488.html

Platts, K. W., & Song, N. (2010). Overseas sourcing decisions—The total cost of sourcing from China. *Supply Chain Management: An International Journal 15*(4), 320–331.

Prahalad, C. K., & Ramaswamy, V. (2004). Co-creation experiences: The next practice in value creation. *Journal of Interactive Marketing 18*(3), 5–14.

Presutti, W. D., Jr., & Mawhinney, J. R. (2009). The value chain revisited. *International Journal of Value Chain Management 3*(2), 146–167.

Pretious, M., & Love, M. (2006). Sourcing ethics and the global market: The case of the UK retail clothing sector. *International Journal of Retail & Distribution Management 34*(12), 892–903.

Proctor, J. (2006). Going my way? *APICS Magazine* (March), 27–29.

Quesada, G., Rachamadugu, R., Gonzalez, M., & Martinez, J. L. (2008). Linking order winning and external supply chain integration strategies. *Supply Chain Management: An International Journal 13*(4), 296–303.

Quinn, J. P. (2007). U.S. ports expand. *Supply Chain Management Review 11*(3), 57–59.

Raskin, A. (2003). Who's minding the store? *Business 2.0 4*(1), 70–74.

Rivoli, P. (2009). *The travels of a T-shirt in the global economy.* Hoboken, NJ: John Wiley & Sons.

Robertson, C. J. (2008). Kola Real's low-cost international expansion strategy. *Thunderbird International Business Review 50*(1), 59–70.

Romano, A. M., & Finley, F. (2006). How Ann Taylor put strategic sourcing on the management map. *Supply Chain Management Review 10*(7), 32–40.

Ross, D. F. (2006). The intimate supply chain. *Supply Chain Management Review 10*(5), 50–57.

Saphir, A. W. (2007). C-TPAT coming of age. *APICS Magazine 17*(3), 41–43.

Sari, K. (2007). Exploring the benefits of vendor managed inventory. *International Journal of Physical Distribution & Logistics Management 37*(7), 529–545.

Shawdon, C. (2006). What do global shippers really think? *Supply Chain Management Review 10*(9), 6–9.

Sheffi, Y., & Rice, J. B., Jr. (2005). A supply chain view of the resilient enterprise. *MIT Sloan Management Review 47*(1), 41–48.

Shub, A. N., & Stonebraker, P. W. (2009). The human impact on supply chains: Evaluating the importance of "soft" areas on integration and performance. *Supply Chain Management: An International Journal 14*(1), 31–40.

Siegfried, M. (2011). Tracing through the supply chain. *Inside Supply Management 22*(5), 36–39.

Simatupang, T. M., & Sridharan, R. (2002). The collaborative supply chain. *International Journal of Logistics Management 13*(1), 15–30.

Slone, R. E. (2004). Leading a supply chain turnaround. *Harvard Business Review 82*(10), 114–121.

Steermann, H. (2003). A practical look at CPFR®: The Sears-Michelin experience. *Supply Chain Management Review 7*(4), 46–53.

Su, J. C. P., Chang, Y.-L., & Ferguson, M. (2005). Evaluation of postponement structures to accommodate mass customization. *Journal of Operations Management 23*, 305–318.

Taleb, N. N. (2010). *The black swan.* New York, NY: Random House.

Tang, C. S. (2006). Perspectives in supply chain risk management. *International Journal of Production Economics 103*, 451–488.

Ting, S.-C., & Cho, D. I. (2008). An integrated approach for supplier selection and purchasing decisions. *Supply Chain Management: An International Journal 13*(2), 116–127.

Trent, R. J., & Monczka, R. M. (2005). Achieving excellence in global sourcing. *MIT Sloan Management Review 47*(1), 24–32.

Tsay, A. A., Nahmias, S., & Agrawal, N. (1999). Modeling supply chain contracts: A review. In S. Tayur, R. Ganeshan, & M. Magazine (Eds.), *Quantitative models for supply chain management* (pp. 299–336). Norwell, MA: Kluwer Academic.

Van Hoek, R. I., & Mitchell, A. J. (2006). The challenge of internal misalignment. *International Journal of Logistics: Research and Applications 9*(3), 269–281.

Vanek, F. M., & Smith, R. I. (2004). Prospects for rail freight from the peripheral regions: The case of north-east Scotland and Grampian Country Foods. *International Journal of Logistics: Research and Applications 7*(1), 59–70.

Vizio. (2011). *About Vizio.* Retrieved June 16, 2011, from Vizio: http://www.vizio.com/about

Wagner, S. M. (2006). Supplier development practices: An exploratory study. *European Journal of Marketing 40*(5/6), 554–571.

Wahyuni, S., Ghauri, P., & Karsten, L. (2007). Managing international strategic alliance relationships. *Thunderbird International Business Review 49*(6), 671–687.

Wang, J. (2007). Logistics in China. In D. Waters (Ed.), *Global logistics* (5th ed., pp. 391–402). London, UK: Kogan Page.

Watts, C. A., & Hahn, C. K. (1993). Supplier development programs: An empirical analysis. *International Journal of Purchasing and Materials Management 29*(2), 10–17.

Weitzman, H. (2011, July 19). Boeing's 787 ready for take-off after three-year delay. *Financial Times*, p. 22.

Wilson, R. (2011). 22nd annual CSCMP state of logistics report. Retrieved July 26, 2011, from CSCMP: http://cscmp.org/memberonly/state.asp

Wu, H. J., & Dunn, S. C. (1995). Environmentally responsible logistics systems. *International Journal of Physical Distribution & Logistics Management 25*(2), 20–38.

Young, R. R., Swan, P. F., Thomchick, E. A., & Ruamsook, K. (2009). Extending landed cost models to improve offshore sourcing decisions. *International Journal of Physical Distribution & Logistics Management 39*(4), 320–335.

Yung, I.-S., Lee, H.-W., & Lai, M.-H. (2009). Competitive advantages created by a cluster collaboration network for supplier management in notebook PC production. *Total Quality Management 20*(7), 763–775.

Index

Note: Page numbers followed by an *e* refer to examples.

Announcing the Business Expert Press Digital Library

Concise E-books Business Students
Need for Classroom and Research

This book can also be purchased in an e-book collection by your library as

- a one-time purchase,
- that is owned forever,
- allows for simultaneous readers,
- has no restrictions on printing,
- can be downloaded as PDFs from within the library community.

Our digital library collections are a great solution to beat the rising cost of textbooks. E-books can be loaded into their course management systems or onto students' e-book readers.

The **Business Expert Press** digital libraries are very affordable, with no obligation to buy in future years.

For more information, please visit **www.businessexpertpress.com/librarians**. To set up a trial in the United States, please contact **Sheri Dean** at sheri.dean@globalepress.com; for all other regions, contact **Nicole Lee** at nicole.lee@igroupnet.com.

OTHER TITLES IN OUR SUPPLY AND OPERATIONS MANAGEMENT COLLECTION
Series Editor: **Steven Nahmias,** *Santa Clara University*

- *Production Line Efficiency: A Comprehensive Guide for Managers* by Sabry Shaaban
- *Transforming US Army Supply Chains: Strategies for Management Innovation* by Greg Parlier
- *Design, Analysis and Optimization of Supply Chains: A System Dynamics Approach* by William R. Killingsworth
- *Supply Chain Planning and Analytics: The Right Product in the Right Place at the Right Time The Right Product in the Right Place at the Right Time* by Gerald Feigin
- *Supply-Chain Survival in the Age of Globalization* by James A. Pope
- *Better Business Decisions Using Cost Modeling: For Procurement, Operations, and Supply Chain Professionals* by Victor E. Sower

CPSIA information can be obtained at www.ICGtesting.com
Printed in the USA
BVOW08s2032120714

358845BV00004B/5/P